THE
1960s
SCRAPBOOK

THE 1960s SCRAPBOOK

ANGELA DODSON

MAGNA BOOKS

Published by Magna Books
Magna Road
Wigston
Leicester LE18 4ZH

Produced by Bison Books Ltd
Kimbolton House
117A Fulham Road
London SW3 6RL

ISBN 1-85422-213-9

Printed in Slovenia

Page 1: An American soldier in Vietnam armed with an M60
machine gun.

Page 2: Jimi Hendrix.

Below, left to right: A selection of magazine covers showing
some of the most memorable people and events of the decade.

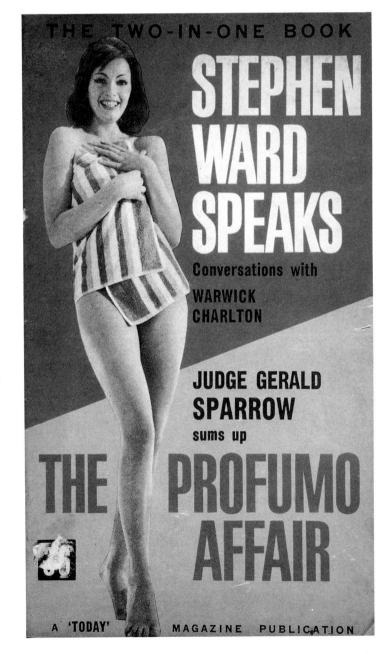

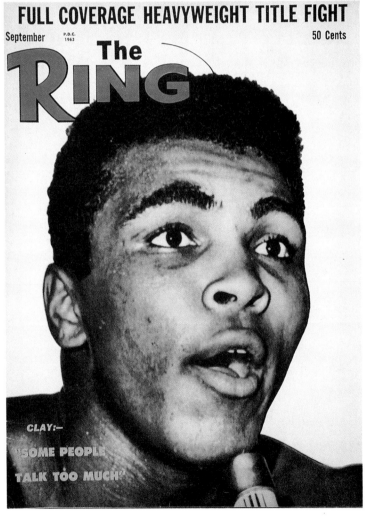

Contents

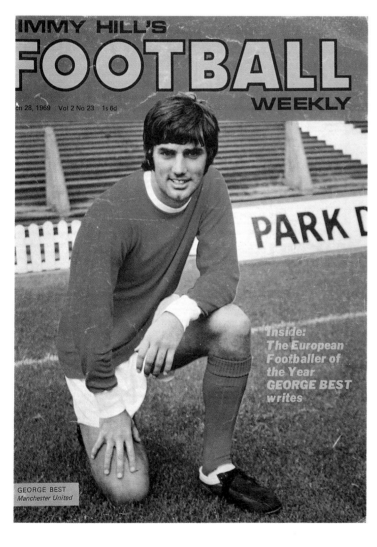

JIMMY HILL'S
FOOTBALL WEEKLY

n 28, 1969 Vol 2 No 23 1s 6d

PARK D

Inside:
The European
Footballer of
the Year
GEORGE BEST
writes

GEORGE BEST
Manchester United

Newsweek

OCTOBER 30, 1967

TROUBLE IN HIPPIELAND

Introduction

The sixties – the years of flower power and hippies, war and assassination, great music and free love – has embedded itself in the popular memory. No other decade has captured the imagination of succeeding generations so strongly.

Superficially, the decade of sex and drugs and rock'n'roll seems like one long party, broken occasionally by the odd protest march, or briefly soured by the assassination of a popular public figure. Life may have been like that for many, probably those who still remark that if you can remember the sixties, you weren't really there. Some of the most memorable images are those of battle-scarred troops in Vietnam, and one of the most frequently shown pieces of film records the final moments of President Kennedy in Dallas in 1963 as he was felled by the assassin's bullet. The murder of political figures such as the Kennedy brothers, Martin Luther King, and Malcolm X were events that contradict the image of the peaceful, laidback decade.

The bomb, an emotive issue from the 1950s onward, continued to provoke debate and protest during the sixties. The Superpowers came closer than ever to total war in the early years of the decade, and spent the rest of the time arming and encouraging conflicts between smaller nations.

War was just one of the issues that brought concerned individuals out on to the streets to protest. None of the Johnson Administration could travel anywhere without meeting a crowd of angry, placard-carrying protestors, and the war

inspired sit-ins and marches throughout the western world. Students in Paris brought the city, and nearly the whole of France to a standstill during the *événements* of 1968 as they clashed with police in bloody riots that shocked the country. De Gaulle regained control with difficulty.

Another contentious issue in the USA was that of civil rights. In 1960 racial segregation was rigidly enforced across the southern states; many restaurants barred black diners, schools were segregated and blacks in many areas were prevented from registering as voters. The threat of integration imposed by Washington provoked a resurgency in the strength of the Ku Klux Klan and many black people lived in a constant state of fear. John Kennedy identified himself with the civil rights movement during his presidential campaign, but it was not until 1964, after several years of bitter struggle and dignified protest that President Johnson signed the Civil Rights Act, and even this did not end the racial conflict. The charismatic Martin Luther King, perished in 1968, his violent death provoking riots across America.

Governments generally reacted defensively and guardedly to this new age of popular protest. There were surely more marches, riots and protests during the 1960s than in any other decade until that time. The idealism of the early years of the decade under Kennedy dissipated after 1963 in the USA, at least. America became embroiled in an unpopular and costly war which tended to overshadow the rest of the decade. In France political debate, first over Algeria, and later over the student unrest of 1968, occupied the French political arena. Macmillan's Conservative government, widely perceived to be out of touch, was replaced by the (comparitively) exciting Labour party under Harold Wilson, who promised that Britain would be remade 'in the white heat of the technological revolution.' The contrast between Britain and America in the middle years of the decade could not have been greater: America was engulfed in controversy and doubt: in Britain the keynote was optimism, progress and even fun.

Philip Larkin dated the dawn of the swinging sixties to 1963. Four lads from Liverpool helped revolutionize popular music: Beatlemania swamped Britain then and barely abated for six years. The Beatles were just one part of the radical change that overcame youth culture. As the decade wore on, hair got longer as skirts grew shorter, attitudes to sex became less stuffy, the Women's Movement improved the lot of many women, and people began to take stimulants harder (and often more dangerous) than mere alcohol. Hippies preached the power of love, and 'Be-ins', 'Love-ins' and pop festivals became common occurrences during the summers at the end of the decade. Golden Gate Park in San Francisco hosted the first be-in, which was presided over by Allen Ginsberg. Hippy counter-culture gradually took over from irreverent British pop culture and reached its apogee during 1967's Summer of Love.

The cross fertilization between the various areas of the arts was remarkable: psychedelia penetrated the worlds of fashion, art and pop, as well as hippies' minds. Pop stars, many of whom had started out at art college (John Lennon, Keith Richards and Eric Clapton, to name a few), mixed with writers, artists and intellectuals. Pop art showed clearly the link between commercial youth culture and the art world.

It is almost impossible to make sense of a decade that thrived on such disparate influences. The sixties made a lasting impact on popular culture and mores, and the influence of the decade is still felt today.

Previous pages: One of the most memorable and horrifying images of the decade. A South Vietnamese officer shoots a Viet Cong soldier at point-blank range in Saigon, February 1968.

Left: Harold Macmillan, British Prime Minister 1957-63, who coined the phrase 'You've never had it so good'.

Right: Dwight D Eisenhower, President of the USA, 1952-60. A popular and successful general during World War II, 'Ike' presided over a period of unparalleled prosperity in America, but by 1960 seemed old and a little out of touch.

Below: Greensborough, North Carolina, 1960. Four black students defied the laws of racial segregation by eating in a whites-only café. Their protest was the first of many.

MOST DRAMATIC DEBUT OF 1959: NEWEST EDITION OF THE LINCOLN LOOK

A masterpiece at rest... A miracle in motion

Classic beauty, unexcelled craftsmanship... THE 1959 LINCOLN LOOK

LINCOLN DIVISION, FORD MOTOR COMPANY

Images of a decade waiting to happen.

Left: This car advertisement is a clear indicator of American aspirations. The inhabitants of the richest nation on earth naturally drove the largest cars possible.

Below far left: 2 March 1960 – a great day for millions of fans. Sergeant Elvis Presley returned home from his National Service in Germany to a rapturous welcome. At this time he was unrivaled as the 'King of rock 'n' roll,' though it would not be long before new voices rose to challenge him.

Below left: French paratroopers drop into the besieged fortress of Dien Bien Phu in 1954. The besieging Viet Minh were later to force the French out of IndoChina, leaving the country torn between Ho Chi Minh's Communist forces and the Nationalist supporters of Ngo Dinh Diem. In 1956 IndoChina was divided in two: North Vietnam and South Vietnam.

Right: The sentiments expressed in this classic pop art poster would have shocked many more people at the beginning of the decade than it did at the end.

Below: Fidel Castro, the personification of the 'red menace,' addresses the UN in 1960.

Below right: Allen Ginsberg (left) and Timothy Leary, the great performance gurus of the sixties. A 'beat' poet of note, Ginsberg was proud that he had achieved the introduction of the word 'fuck' into texts studied in schools. Leary, a college professor, was introduced to LSD in 1962, and spent much of the decade experimenting with mind-expanding drugs.

Above, left and right: The foreign policy of the United States in the late 1950s was dominated by the 'Cold War' with the Soviet Union. The USA and her allies dreaded the expansion of Communism at the expense of the mainly Western, capitalist democracies, and saw 'the bomb,' or nuclear deterrent, as the ultimate preventative. The leader of the Soviet Union, Nikita Khrushchev (left) was an amiable and flamboyant politician who had done much to dispel western fears about the Communist bogey. He was, however, notoriously unpredictable, and his attitude to the USA swung from threats of 'burying capitalism,' to preaching 'peaceful coexistence.' With such a mercurial opponent, the leaders of the Western world believed that possession of a nuclear deterrent was justified, but not everyone agreed. In Britain the Campaign for Nuclear Disarmament enjoyed strong support, and organized an annual ban-the-bomb march from the Aldermaston Atomic Weapons Research Establishment to London (above). In the USA the National Committee for a Sane Nuclear Policy taught citizens about civil defense (right).

HEADLINES I:
From Camelot to Vietnam

The period 1960-63 is often nostalgically termed the 'Camelot' or 'Kennedy' years. Young, committed and charismatic, John Fitzgerald Kennedy set the tone for the high-flown idealism of the new US administration in his inaugural address of 20 January 1961: 'Ask not what your country can do for you but what you can do for your country.' One of the first manifestations of the Kennedy commitment to human rights was the establishment of the Peace Corps, which sent young, enthusiastic volunteers to aid the Third World.

The Third World was still largely under Western influence, despite Soviet aid and arms programs. On 3 February 1960, British Prime Minister Harold Macmillan made his famous 'Winds of change' speech to the South African Parliament: 'The most striking of all the impressions I have formed since I left London a month ago is the strength of African national consciousness. It is happening everywhere. The wind of change is blowing through the continent.' The process of granting independence to former colonies had begun after World War II, but the pace of and pressure for decolonization increased vastly in the 1960s. Nearly 20 newly independent states were created in 1960 alone, although the response of the minority South African government was increased repression, leading to the Sharpeville Massacre.

Ghana, the former Gold Coast, was the first black West African country to achieve independence, becoming an independent dominion within the British Commonwealth in 1957 and a republic in 1960. This overall pattern was repeated in the rest of the region, although in Nigeria tribal and regional divisions led to the temporary secession of the Ibo people and the Biafran War, which ended only in 1970.

The worst problems, however, were in the Belgian Congo, where a sudden change of policy by the imperial power launched the Congolese into independence with little or no preparation. The other problem area was Algeria, which was a French province rather than a protectorate like Morocco or Tunisia, and which had a large settler population that wished to remain French. The resulting crisis led to the fall of the Fourth Republic in France itself in 1958 and a series of attempted military coups in Algeria before independence was finally proclaimed in 1962.

The increasingly hostile relations between the USA and USSR during the 1950s hit a new low in 1960 with the U2 sky-plane scandal, which gave the flamboyant and upredictable Soviet premier Nikita Khrushchev a golden opportunity to humiliate the rival superpower. Foreign policy was a major issue in the American presidential election later that year; the Kennedy Democrats were committed to closing the supposed nuclear gap with the Soviet Union, and to taking a tough line with the revolutionary government of Fidel Castro in Cuba. In early 1961 Castro aligned himself with the Soviet bloc, and in response Kennedy authorized a covert CIA operation to destabilize the Cuban regime. The expectation that a general uprising would follow the landing of Cuban exiles in the Bay of Pigs proved unfounded, however, and there was no disguising Washington's complicity in the ensuing fiasco.

Khrushchev made it plain that he would defend Cuba in the event of another attack, but also gave assurances that the Russians would not establish military bases of their own there. This was consistent with general Soviet policy; even in

Eastern Europe the Russians had refrained from installing offensive nuclear missiles, despite America's nuclear presence in Western Eurpe and Turkey. In October 1962, however, American spy flights over Cuba revealed missiles in place at a newly constructed missile site. The resulting confrontation brought the two superpowers to the verge of open hostilities, and world nuclear war threatened. After eight days of brinkmanship, Khrushchev agreed to remove the missiles in return for a guarantee of Cuban sovereignty.

The other focus of Soviet-American tension in the early 1960s lay in the heart of Europe. Berlin, deep inside the Communist German Democratic Republic, was still run as a single free city by the four wartime allies, Russia, America, France and Britain. As the economic gap between Communist East and capitalist West Germany widened, growing numbers of East Germans used Berlin as an escape route to the West. On 6 August 1961 alone, 2035 people crossed from East to West Berlin. The Communist response, on 13 August, was to seal the border, first with barbed wire, then with a permanent wall eight feet high, finally with a vast fortification 100 meters wide. The Berlin Wall became, for nearly 30 years, the symbol of a divided world. As a *fait accompli*, however, the Wall stabilized a potentially inflammable situation; individuals died, but there were no more Berlin crises.

Only five months after his stand for freedom in Berlin, Kennedy was killed by an assassin's bullet in Dallas, Texas. His successor, Lyndon Johnson, was at least as committed a liberal as his predecessor, but his dream of building a 'Great Society' was pre-empted by a war that was to tear the US apart. The Camelot years were over.

"... and friends?"

Previous pages: The Kennedys descend the steps of Airforce One at Dallas, 22 November 1963.

Left: A US Navy patrol plane hovers over a Soviet freighter in the Caribbean, while USS *Barry* pulls alongside to investigate the cargo. The Soviet Union was suspected of supplying Cuba with missiles, and the crisis of 1962 brought the world dangerously close to war.

Above: A 1961 cartoon from the British satirical magazine *Punch*, relating to the EEC. President de Gaulle of France, aware of the close diplomatic ties between Britain and the USA, believed that British entry into the Common Market would increase American influence in Europe. For this reason he was reluctant to admit Britain to full membership of the EEC.

Right: Churchill's metaphorical 'iron curtain' became a concrete reality in 1961 with the construction of the Berlin Wall.

Left and above: Domestic politics in the United States in the early 1960s were dominated by one man: John Fitzgerald Kennedy. More than any other politician, JFK came to symbolize the youthful optimism of the era, which was a little ironic, given his own personal cynicism and worldliness. The Kennedy family, rich East Coast Catholics with ambitious political aspirations, were no strangers to the world of politics. Joseph Kennedy, the founder of the family fortune, and father of John and Robert, had been US ambassador to Britain during World War II. Elected as the Democratic Presidential candidate in 1960, John Kennedy had an impeccable pedigree. He was a decorated war hero, a Pulitzer Prize winner and had represented his home state of Massachusetts at Congressional or Senatorial level since 1947. Kennedy was not, however, a particularly popular candidate within his own party. Many mistrusted him for being young, rich and Catholic, and he patently lacked the moral convictions of

Adlai Stevenson, the candidate favored by the left of the party. His campaign focused on Eisenhower's perceived weakness in foreign policy; Kennedy pledged to take a tougher line against the Soviet Union and its acolytes, particularly Castro in Cuba. The Presidential campaign itself very quickly became a matter of image. While Kennedy was immensely photogenic, Nixon (above right) had a permanent 'five o'clock shadow' and shifty eyes. The televized debate between the candidates, the first of its kind, emphasized these impressions and Nixon lost the election, although only just. Kennedy may only have achieved victory with a tiny 19,000 majority (which was probably rigged in Illinois), but it won him the White House. His inaugural address on 20 January 1961 (left) inspired his listeners. The famous 'Ask not what your country can do for you, but what you can do for your country,' captured the imagination of a nation and launched America on the surge of the 'Camelot years.'

These pages: Kennedy surrounded himself with an articulate and highly-educated governing elite, including his brother Robert (left) who became Attorny General in 1961. The idealistic rhetoric of the early months of the Kennedy administration barely disguised his pugnacious foreign policy. He pumped an extra $17 billion into arms spending, accelerating the nuclear arms race, but he also realized that the Soviet Union was not the only threat to world peace. Following General Maxwell Taylor's beliefs that Communism could spread like a scourge throughout the Third World, unless the USA intervened with counter-insurgensy forces, Kennedy announced the creation of the Green Berets, an élite body, designed to act as a rapid-reaction force in areas threatened by the 'red menace.'

Left: British Prime Minister Harold Macmillan, and below left, Hugh Gaitskill, the leader of the Labour Party. Once described as a 'dessicated calculating machine,' Gaitskill was an extremely able politician, whose influence pervaded the Labour Party long after his death in 1963.

Right and below: It was evident at the beginning of the 1960s that Britain's imperial glory was severely diminished as increasing numbers of its colonies gained independence. In Yemen (right), the former premier, Abdel Qawee Mackakee, trained with anti-British guerrillas during the emergency of 1961.

Below: Queen Elizabeth II with Commonwealth Prime Ministers in 1962. In 1960 Macmillan declared in a speech to the South African Parliament that 'the wind of change is blowing through the continent,' meaning that Britain would not resist the trend towards independence in the colonies. Once they had attained independence, many retained their links with Britain, with the Queen as head of state, throughout the Commonwealth.

Left: (main picture) Lieutenant Alexander Nyirenda lights a torch on the summit of Mount Kilimanjaro in Tanganyika to celebrate his country's independence as Tanzania on 9 December, 1961; (inset) Jomo Kenyatta waves his ceremonial fly whisk as he arrives at London Airport a month earlier, to negotiate Kenya's independence.

Above: The white minority South African government responded with ruthless repression to black demands for free expression and the right to organize politically. On 21 March 1960, in Sharpeville, South African police fired on a crowd of black demonstrators, killing 70 and wounding over 200. The violence only served to exacerbate the situation; the following month the two most important black organizations, the African National Congress and the Pan Africanist Congress, were outlawed.

Right: Throughout the 1960s rebel movements struggled to overthrow Portuguese colonial rule in Angola.

Left: In the Congo the handover of power from the Belgians to local black Africans was far from smooth, due to Belgian failure to groom a native élite capable of self-government. Independence was rushed through on 30 June 1960; here Patrice Lumumba, the new Prime Minister, and Belgian premier Gaston Eyskens sign the act of independence in Leopoldville.

Below left: The new flag of the Republic of the Congo is carried round the arena of the Baudouin stadium to celebrate independence.

Right: Independence was almost immediately followed by the disintegration of the country; the province of Katanga, led by Moise Tshombe, seceded and Lumumba's government requested UN assistance to restore unity. Here Tshombe is chaired by supporters on his release from detention in 1961, after agreeing to abandon plans for an independent Katanga.

Below: Demonstrators demand the release of Lumumba after his deposition in January 1961. He had alienated Western interests by approaching the USSR for help.

Below and below right: In Algeria the movement for independence from France provoked an intense reaction from French settlers, who in January 1960 erected barricades and attempted a military takeover to ensure Algeria remained French.

Right: When peace talks between Paris and the provisional Algerian government were agreed in 1961, French generals established the OAS (Organisation de l'Armée Secrète) and staged an uprising in April. Here paratroopers hold back the crowds of European settlers who have come to hear the generals speak. The rebellion lasted four days.

Far right: General de Gaulle, who had become French premier in 1958, was determined on a compromise solution in Algeria.

Far left above: The OAS waged a campaign of terror in Paris in their efforts to prevent Algerian independence; this car bomb in January 1962 was detonated near the French Foreign Office in the Quai d'Orsay.

Left and far left below: The Front de Libération Nationale (FLN) first launched an armed uprising in pursuit of Algerian independence in 1954, under the leadership of Ahmed Ben Bella.

Above: Independence day celebrations on 1 July 1962.

Right: In 1963 Ben Bella was elected first president of Algeria and legalized the expropriation of most foreign-owned land and many business enterprises. Here Muslim women in traditional dress press forward to give their jewelry in response to Ben Bella's appeal for valuables as a contribution to the national budget.

The start of the new decade saw a slight easing in the Cold War between capitalist and Communist countries, but a conference of the four major world powers, in May 1960 was jeopardized by the U2 spyplane scandal. On 1 May a US pilot, Gary Powers (*above*), took off from a Turkish airfield for a routine spy flight over the Soviet Union and was shot down by a Soviet anti-aircraft missile.

Above left: The altitude and speed of the U2 was supposed to make it invulnerable to missile defenses.

Left: Russian leader Nikita Khrushchev exploited the incident to the full by postponing the announcement of Powers' capture until the eve of the Paris summit, by which time President Eisenhower, assuming that Powers was dead, had denied that the aircraft was on an espionage mission. Here Khrushchev pounds the table at the opening of the 15th General Assembly of the UN in October 1960.

Above right: Eisenhower addresses the nation on his return from the Paris summit; nothing was achieved and superpower relations hit a new low. Powers was put on trial in August and sentenced to ten years imprisonment, but was exchanged in 1962 for a Soviet spy.

Right: Another spy scandal hit the news headlines again in 1962, with rumors that Guy Burgess and Donald Maclean, British diplomats who had spied for the Russians and escaped to the USSR in 1951, were on the move and would soon be recaptured.

The Cuban missile crisis in October 1962 brought the USA and the USSR to the brink of armed confrontation for the second time within 18 months. The disastrous American landing at the Bay of Pigs in April 1961, in the expectation of a Cuban revolution that never happened, tempted the Russians to establish a larger presence in Cuba. In July 1962 US spyplanes detected an increase in Soviet shipments to Cuba, and on 14 October aerial photographs revealed an offensive missile base under construction.

Left: President Kennedy pictured with U2 pilots, whose spy flights over Cuba were vastly increased in September 1962.

Below: The US shows the UN Security Council its aerial photographs proving the existence of Soviet missile bases in Cuba. On the following day a rambling message from Khrushchev marked the first stage in the Russian climb-down.

Right: On 22 October Kennedy had announced a naval blockade. Nineteen US naval vessels moved into position off Cuba and 12 of the 25 Russian ships traveling to Cuba either halted or altered course.

Below right: One of the aerial reconnaissance photographs of missile bases under construction which precipitated the confrontation.

KASIMOV

17 OCTOBER 1962

CAMILO CIENFUEGOS (SANTA CLARA) AIRFIELD
22-29N 79-55W

N

16 FISHBEDS

9 FAGOTS

12 FISHBEDS

9 FAGOTS

AGOTS

3 LIAISONS

11 FISHBEDS

A/C CRATES

Berlin proved another conflagration point in East/West relations, and in August 1961 Soviet guards sealed off the border between East and West Berlin. By 1963, when Kennedy visited Berlin (*left*), the Berlin Wall was a reality; 41 people had already died (*inset*) trying to cross it.

Above: The wall marches past the famous Brandenburg Gate. It instantly became a vivid symbol of a divided Europe.

Below: West Berliners in the French sector try to maintain contact with the other side in September 1961. The Wall soon became much too high and solid to wave across.

Above left: Ghana had moved relatively peacefully toward independence from Britain in the course of the 1950s. Here President Kwame Nkrumah meets Mao Tse-Tung as part of China's policy of carving out an influential rôle among Africa's newly independent states.

Below left: The USSR was also concerned to extend its power bloc. In 1960 Khrushchev met Presidents Nasser of Egypt and Tito of Yugoslavia at the Russian consulate in New York City.

Above right: Pictured at a special meeting of the UN Afro-Asian block in October 1960 are (from left) Prime Minister Saeb Salaam of Lebanon, Nasser, Nkrumah, Burmese UN ambassador U Thant and Indian Prime Minister Jawaharlal Nehru. The meeting backed a proposal for a meeting between Eisenhower and Khrushchev.

Below right: More diplomacy: the Chinese premier Chou En-Lai is shown garlanded with flowers and being greeted by Nehru at the start of week-long talks about Sino-Indian border disputes.

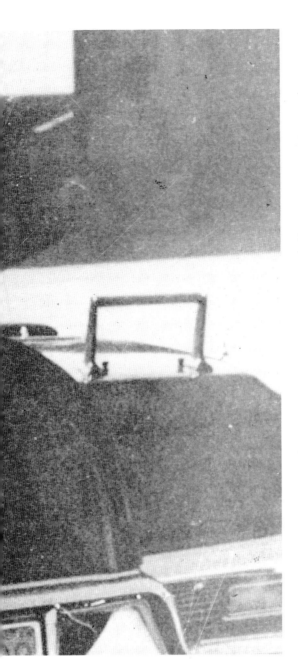

DAILY ● NEWS
NEW YORK'S PICTURE NEWSPAPER ®

ELECTION FINAL

7¢
10¢ OUTSIDE L. I. AND SUBURBS

Vol. 46. No. 113 Copt 1964 News Syndicate Co Inc. New York, N.Y. 10017, Wednesday, November 4, 1964* WEATHER: Sunny and pleasant.

LBJ WINS BIG

Kennedy Senator, Swamps Keating

Left above: The assassin's bullet that changed the world; on 22 November 1963 Jackie Kennedy bends over the dying President Kennedy in Dallas, Texas.

Far left: Vice-President Lyndon Johnson is sworn in as the new president on board the presidential plane.

Left: Kennedy's funeral cortege leaves the White House.

Right: In June 1964 Senator Barry Goldwater triumphs in the critical Californian primary on his way to the Republican presidential nomination.

Above: In November, however, Johnson wins the presidential election with a landslide 41 million votes to Goldwater's 26 million. Although he had none of Kennedy's glamour or sophistication, Johnson was an experienced and effective politician with a strong commitment to civil rights and social reform. This was the high point of American liberalism.

Above left: UN Secretary-General Dag Hammarskjöld gives a press conference in May 1961. In September he flew to the Congo to try and negotiate a peaceful end to the Katangan secession; his plane mysteriously crashed on a flight to Northern Rhodesia, killing all on board.

Above right: U Thant is sworn in as acting Secretary-General after Hammarskjöld's death.

Below: US Secretary of State Dean Rusk, Soviet Foreign Minister Andrei Gromyko and British Foreign Secretary Lord Home sign the first nuclear test ban treaty on 5 August 1963. Brokered by the UN Secretary-General U Thant, and partly a response to the Cuban missile crisis of the previous year, the treaty proscribed nuclear tests in the atmosphere or underwater.

Right: The arms race continued throughout the 1960s, however; here Polaris submarine USS *Henry Clay* demonstrates that missiles could be launched from the surface as well as from a submerged position.

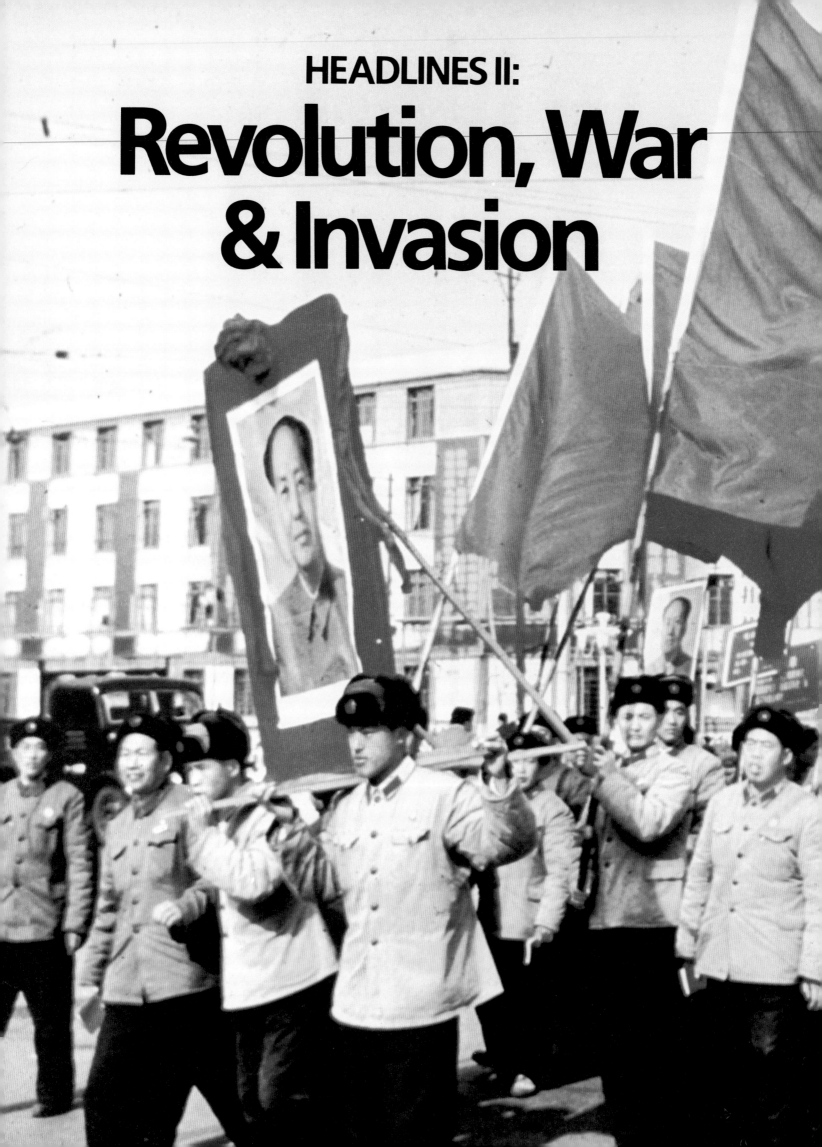

HEADLINES II:
Revolution, War & Invasion

The second half of the 1960s, even more than the first, was a period of turmoil and conflict on the world stage. Within the Eastern bloc, systemic weaknesses revealed the contradictions inherent within the Communist dream, and the process of liberalization in Poland and, more particularly, Czechoslovakia, was ruthlessly suppressed. China emerged into the limelight from a period of political and economic reconstruction which began with the Great Leap Forward in 1958, officially a program to increase productivity while reducing the importance of the bureaucracy. The US, having been forced to accept Castro's Cuban Revolution, responded with direct and immediate military action when, in April 1965, reformists launched an armed uprising in the Dominican Republic. Combined with the Johnson administration's decision in February 1965 to escalate the Vietnam War, this set the scene for five years of confrontation and intervention.

Again the Third World provided a forum for superpower rivalry, this time between Russia and China. The Great Leap Forward and the rising influence of the Maoists meant a corresponding decline in Russia's influence within China. The Sino-Soviet split was confirmed by the Himalayan War of 1962, when Russia supported India against China's border incursions. The military coup in Indonesia in 1965 was motivated by suspicion of President Sukarno's increasingly close ties with China. Mao Tse-Tung's Cultural Revolution, which began in 1965 and spread nationwide in 1966, represented Mao's determination to avoid the damaging social trends associated by many with Russian Communism, as well as a

means of disabling his many and varied political enemies.

1965 was also notable in Africa for Rhodesia's unilateral declaration of independence. The failure of the Central African Federation, with Nyasaland and Northern Rhodesia becoming the independent states of Malawi and Zambia respectively in 1964, gave white supremacists in Southern Rhodesia total control. After intense negotiations with British Prime Minister Harold Wilson failed in late 1966, the UN voted mandatory sanctions against the breakaway state.

In 1967 another long-running problem boiled over, this time in the Middle East. Since Israel's declaration of independence in 1948 there had already been two Arab-Israeli Wars, in 1947-49 and the Suez Crisis in 1956. In 1967 defeated the combined forces of Egypt, Syria and Jordan.

The contradictions within the Soviet system became increasingly clear in the late 1960s; some experts described the Iron Curtain countries as 'post-revolutionary', suggesting that they were neither capitalist nor socialist. The reality of socialist revolution, as Mao saw only too clearly, was that a bureaucratic ruling class controlled the economy and politics. In a system of guaranteed employment there was little incentive to increase productivity, and rates of growth were declining throughout the Eastern bloc. The less rigidly controlled state of Czechoslovakia tried decentralizing economic decision-making and providing greater incentives to labor. Economic reform in turn led to popular demands for political change, and the Warsaw Pact decided to intervene; the Prague Spring suffered early frostbite.

Previous pages: Red Guards carrying a portrait of Mao Tse-Tung parade in Peking during the Cultural Revolution.

Left: The Middle East was the focus for perhaps the sharpest superpower rivalry in the Third World. In the mid-1960s a new arms race began, with the Russians supplying Egypt and the Americans the Israelis. Israel's lightning victory in the Six-Day War in June 1967 was very popular in the West but contained the seeds of future conflict. Here Defense Minister General Moshe Dayan, Yitzhak Rabin and General Uzi Narkiss enter the Old City of Jerusalem.

Above right: After the fall of Khrushchev in 1964, new premier Leonid Brezhnev (center) set out to restore the absolute control of the Communist Party over Soviet culture and to crush any tentative signs of dissent.

Below right: US Vice-President Hubert Humphrey is greeted by placards protesting the Vietnam War as he electioneers in 1968.

Left: The funeral of Sir Winston Churchill in 1965 was a pageant of former imperial glory, pointing up the rapid pace of change.

Below: At the dedication of the John F Kennedy Memorial in Runnymede, England, former Prime Minister Harold Macmillan addresses the gathering. Jacqueline Kennedy is seated to his left, with Queen Elizabeth and Prince Philip beyond her, while Robert and Edward Kennedy are behind.

Right: In Britain the sixties was a decade of largely Labour government. The small Labour majority in the October 1964, election which brought Harold Wilson to power, was transformed into a landslide victory in 1966. The promise of a white-hot technological revolution proved illusory, however; Britain was falling behind her main industrial competitors in modernization and productivity.

Below right: Wilson and the leader of the Conservative opposition, Edward Heath, are pictured in 1968 at a celebration of the 50th anniversary of the enfranchising of British women.

REDPATH BROWN & CO LTD
CONSTRUCTIONAL ENGINEERS & STEEL MERCHANTS

Left: Archbishop Makarios, President of Cyprus, is welcomed to the UN in New York by Secretary-General U Thant. Cyprus had gained independence from Britain in 1960, but in 1964 the UN had to intervene to end hostilities between Greek and Turkish Cypriots.

Below left: Ian Smith, Prime Minister of the British colony of Southern Rhodesia, signs the unilateral declaration of independence (UDI) on 27 November 1965, in an attempt to ensure the continued supremacy of the white minority.

Right: African representatives walk out of the UN in protest at British policy regarding Rhodesia.

Below right: On the fourth anniversary of UDI, in 1969, demonstrators clash with police outside Rhodesia House in London.

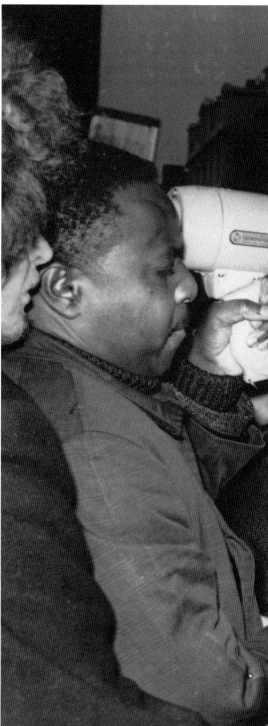

Left: The American domestic scene in the mid-1960s was dominated by anti-war protest, particularly among the student population, and the race issue. At the end of 1966 the Republican ex-actor Ronald Reagan won the governorship of California on a law-and-order ticket, promising to restore discipline on the Berkeley campus.

Below: President Johnson meets his Attorney General and Secretary of Defense to discuss the Detroit race riots.

Right: The assassination of Robert Kennedy in June 1968 removed the most popular anti-war candidate from the race for the Democratic presidential nomination that year. Johnson had already announced his intention of standing down, but gave only lukewarm support to his vice-president, Hubert Humphrey.

Below right and far right: The winner of the 1968 presidential election was the Republican Richard Nixon, campaigning on a Vietnam 'peace-with-honor' ticket. In 1969 he addressed the UN General Assembly in an attempt to pressure Hanoi into productive peace negotiations.

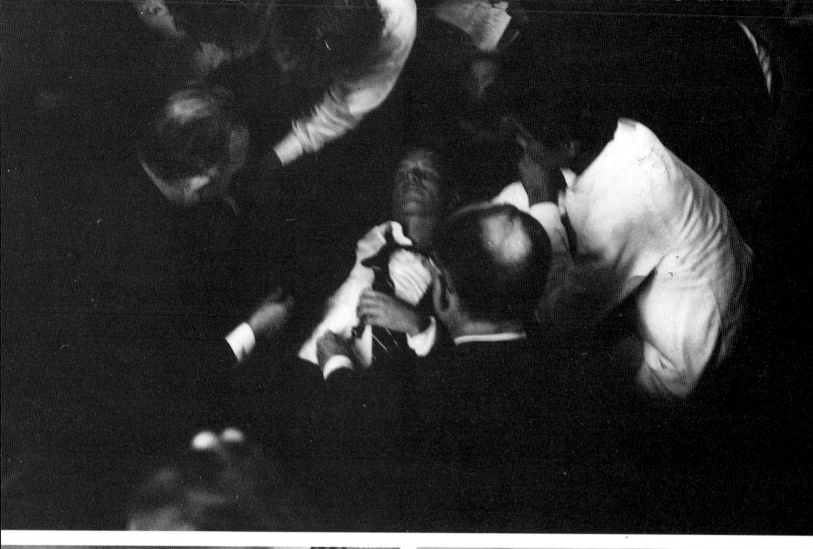

In China the People's Republic proclaimed by Mao Tse-Tung in 1949 underwent radical change in the course of the 1960s. After a period of relative eclipse, Mao reasserted his own authority and also made a decisive bid for leadership of the Third World revolution when he launched the 'Cultural Revolution' inside China in 1965 and called for a 'people's war' to overthrow both American imperialism and the 'socialist imperialism' of Moscow. Determined to prevent the Communist revolution in China solidifying into an authoritarian bureaucracy as in the USSR, Mao selected Chinese youth as his instrument against the power of the urban bourgeoisie.

Above left: The emergence of the Red Guard was the crucial factor in Mao's campaign. Composed largely of middle-school and university students, the Red Guards gave their allegiance to Mao personally rather than to the Communist Party. By mid-June 1966 the whole educational system was in disorder as students flocked to Peking, and even in the autumn the middle schools and universities did not re-open. The Guards instead studied the thoughts of Mao, published in the gnomic *Little Red Book*.

Left: At a vast rally in Peking's Tienanmen Square, Mao's wife Chiang Ching and Chou En-Lai greet the throng.

Above: A young Red Guard distributes leaflets on a Peking street, enforcing the new drive for a stricter adherence to the Communist way of life. Mao urged the Guards to travel through the country and shake up the existing party and government apparatus; the result was chaos. Officials were attacked and paraded through the streets in dunce's caps. Anything linked to the past or the West, such as museums, books and works of art, was destroyed. People were killed in the ensuing violence, and soon the turmoil affected production. As large numbers of the industrial workforce took advantage of the breakdown of law and order to form new trade union organizations, Mao began to turn away from his own revolution.

Left: A procession of Red Guards march through Peking with cymbals and drums and vast red banners.

Top: The 72-year-old Mao swims in the Yangtze River – he reportedly covered eight miles – to prove his eternal youth. 'There was joy that chairman Mao was in such good health,' said the official report.

Above: A young Red Guard chants the slogans written on the placard she carries.

The Six-Day War was a pre-emptive strike by Israel in response to the Egyptian closure of the Straits of Tiran to Israeli shipping.

Left: President Nasser of Egypt and King Hussein of Jordan sign a mutual defense treaty against Israel in May 1967.

Below left: Golda Meir became Israeli Prime Minister in 1969.

Right: Israeli Centurion tanks maneuver in the Negev Desert in the run-up to war in May 1967.

Below: Arab students demonstrate outside the White House.

Left: Israeli tanks advance on the Golan Heights on the border with Syria on 10 June, the day the ceasefire was declared. By then Israel had taken the whole of the Sinai peninsula and the Gaza strip (from Egypt) and the West Bank territories along the Jordan River (previously controlled by Jordan), as well as the strategically important Golan Heights, and was within striking distance of Damascus.

Below left: General Moshe Dayan, Minister of Defense, masterminded the Israeli strategy. The Israelis formed the view that war was inevitable and took the offensive on 5 June by destroying the Egyptian air force on the ground. Without air cover on the Arab side, the war was over in six days.

Right: General Abdul Mohem Hussaini, the Egyptian military governor in Gaza, after his surrender on 7 June.

Below: The outcome of the 1967 war was to give the Israelis some bargaining power over the Arabs for the first time since 1948, but a peace which recognized Israel would also mean solving the Palestinian question within the Arab world, which militated against an early settlement. Instead both sides began to rearm. Here President Nasser pays a surprise visit to Egyptian troops.

Above: In July 1967 President de Gaulle of France arrived in Quebec on a state visit to Canada scheduled to end in the capital, Ottawa. Here he reviews a guard of honor at the dockside.

Left: On 5 August de Gaulle delighted some French Canadians and shocked most of their compatriots by his cry of '*Vive Quebec libre,*' in effect casting his weight behind a separatist revolt by French Canadians.

Right: Former leader of the Canadian Conservative Party John Diefenbaker was one of many Canadian politicians who condemned such interference in Canadian government as 'intolerable.'

Right above: In June 1968 the French-speaking Pierre Trudeau was chosen successor to Prime Minister Lester Pearson.

Far right: In April 1969 de Gaulle lost a domestic referendum and resigned. Here former French premier Georges Pompidou, pre-election favorite, casts his vote in the June presidential election.

De Gaulle's
ECM policy
'wrong' -PM

Port eyes
freeze-up

A JOURNAL

De Gaulle Demands
New Constitution
To 'Free' Quebec

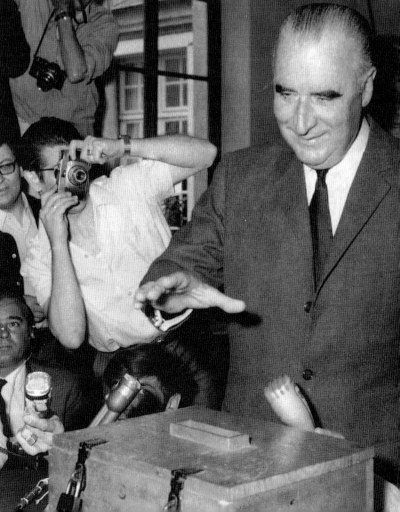

Declining productivity in the Communist-controled Eastern Bloc became an increasing problem in the 1960s and led to some attempts to reform the economic system by decentralizing decision-making. In Czechoslovakia this in turn led to popular demands for political change and, in January 1968, to the installation of a new party chairman, Alexander Dubcek, and widespread political reforms intended to create 'socialism with a human face.' On 20 August, 500,000 Warsaw Pact troops invaded Czechoslovakia.

Left: On 21 August a cross and a pool of blood mark the spot where a young Czech was shot dead during the invasion.

Below left: In the main, Czech resistance was limited to jeering and jostling the invading troops.

Right: Dubcek in May 1968 celebrating the 'Prague Spring'; reform led to an outpouring of cultural activity, political debate and social reorganization.

Below: A tense meeting between Soviet and Czech leaders on 3 August produced what appeared to be a compromise agreement, limiting but accepting reform. Dubcek is pictured on 18 August being greeted by fellow citizens; two days later Russian tanks entered Prague.

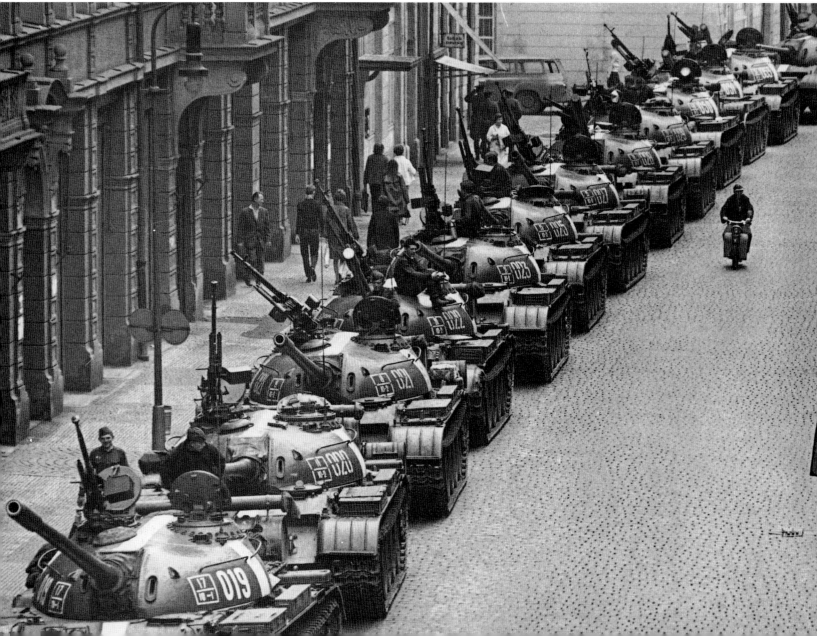

Above left: Czech youths hold a bloodstained Czech flag as tanks rumble past on 21 August.

Below left: A column of Soviet tanks lines a street in Prague Old Town.

Above: The Prague Spring had touched a chord in the free countries of the West. Here a group of Italian students holding their national flag picket the Soviet embassy in protest at the crushing of reform.

Below: Soviet Communist leader Leonid Brezhnev addresses the World Conference of Communist Parties in June 1969, flanked by Prime Minister Alexei Kosygin (left) and President Nikolai Podgorny (right).

Left: UN Secretary-General U Thant visits President de Gaulle at the Elysée Palace in April 1966. They issued a joint statement deploring the bloodshed in Vietnam.

Below left: President Sukarno of Indonesia addresses military leaders after the 1965 military coup which reduced his role to that of figurehead. Real power rested with General Suharto (seated left), who established a military government and became president in 1968.

Right: On 19 December 1968 Generalissimo Francisco Franco, Spanish chief of state, recognized as his legal successor and the future king of Spain, Juan Carlos de Borbón.

Below: Willy Brandt, mayor of Berlin, became in the late 1960s first Foreign Minister and then Chancellor of West Germany, and promoted his *Ostpolitik*, or rapprochement with the Eastern Bloc.

Left: In 1969 Northern Ireland exploded into violence. In January a Catholic civil rights march from Belfast to Londonderry was attacked by militant Protestants, while Protestant Orange Order marches in July and August sparked off Catholic riots in Derry and Belfast. Hooded paramilitary figures like this one paraded openly.

Right: The militant Protestant leader Ian Paisley emerged as a major figure, whipping up Protestant feeling against civil rights for Catholics. In August he met Home Secretary James Callaghan and is seen here leaving the meeting place, pledging 'no surrender' to surrounding newsmen.

Below: Rioting in Londonderry in July 1969; in April the British government had sent troops to Ulster to reinforce the police against growing violence.

Below: One memorable development during the Troubles of Northern Ireland was the election of Bernadette Devlin to the House of Commons. She fought a bitterly contested by-election for an Ulster constituency which had previously returned Unionist members with comfortable majorities. A leader of the student wing of the civil rights movement, Bernadette Devlin was herself a student at the time of the election, and took her seat at the tender age of 21, Britain's youngest parliamentarian. Contrary to the gentlemanly Westminster tradition, she made a fiery and uncompromising maiden speech in a debate on Northern Ireland, provoking a host of congratulatory letters from her parliamentary colleagues.

Right and below right: Riots and marches continued throughout the summer in Ulster, and in August the situation deteriorated beyond control. On 12 August the annual Protestant Apprentice Boys parade in Londonderry sparked off violent clashes between Bogside Catholics on the one hand, and the police and the Protestant B Specials on the other. The violence spread to Belfast, where police drove into Catholic areas firing indiscriminately from armored cars. Eight people were killed, and on 15 August British troops were deployed. The British government regarded the Ulster authorities and the Protestant-dominated police as the prime culprits and pressed for immediate reforms. These proved slow to materialize, however, and in December the Provisional IRA was formed by Republicans who wanted to challenge the British army. The scene was set for a bitter terrorist struggle.

''The picture of the world's greatest superpower killing or seriously injuring 1000 non-combatants a week while trying to pound a tiny, backward nation into submission on an issue whose merits are hotly disputed, is not a pretty one''.
Robert McNamara (Defense Secretary 1964-67) in a letter to LBJ prior to his resignation.
America's involvement in Vietnam began in 1954 as the French withdrew from their former colony, then known as IndoChina. During the 1950s the balance of power on the Vietnamese mainland was a microcosm of the Cold War: the United States supported Diem's government in South Vietnam as a bulwark against the Communist regime of Ho Chi Minh in North Vietnam. From 1959, when Ho Chi Minh began to undermine South Vietnam with guerrilla warfare, American support took the form of sending 'military advisers' to train the South Vietnamese army (the ARVN) in counter-insurgency techniques. By 1963 there were 10,000 such 'advisers' in Vietnam. With the approach of the 1964 US Presidential elections, it was unthinkable that Kennedy or his successor Johnson would withdraw from Southeast Asia. The Republicans would ruthlessly exploit any evidence of foreign policy weakness, and furthermore, it was believed that Communist success in one area would encourage advances elsewhere. The American involvement in Vietnam was complex and controversial; domestic politics were entangled with the almost paranoid fear of Communism that pervaded US foreign policy in the early years of the 1960s.

In 1963 Diem was assassinated during a coup and replaced by Major General Nguyen Khanh. The USA supported him simply because without his leadership, they believed that South Vietnam would fragment into dozens of factions, many of which would unite with the Communists. Two further events in 1964 ensured irrevocable American involvement. Secretary of State Robert McNamara returned from a fact-finding mission recommending increased aid to South Vietnam and by June, the new commander-in-chief, General Westmoreland, controlled 20,000 troops. In August the destroyer USS *Maddox* was attacked in the Gulf of Tonkin while reinforcing South Vietnamese coastal raids in the north. This incident gave President Johnson the excuse he needed to unleash air strikes against North Vietnamese bases. The 'Gulf of Tonkin' Resolution permitted the president to take any necessary measures against hostile action in Vietnam, and the following year the president was able to commit large numbers of troops to the conflict without consulting Congress. With over 80 percent of South Vietnam in Communist hands, the US launched Operation 'Rolling Thunder' in 1965, committing its 180,000 troops to an offensive, rather than merely a defensive role. The USA was determined to justify its actions and involve its allies in the conflict, but despite intense diplomatic efforts, only South Korea, Australia, and New Zealand sent forces. All the Western European powers refused to send reinforcements, and de Gaulle's government openly opposed American policy.

Previous pages: The grim realities of jungle warfare. An airborne division dig-in, 1968.

Left: The architects of the war, US Secretary of Defense, Robert McNamara (right) and General William Westmoreland (left) tour the Demilitarized Zone (DMZ), 1967.

Above right: Ho Chi Minh, the President of North Vietnam. One of the great survivors of southeast Asian politics, Ho had been battling for Vietnamese nationalism since the second world war.

Right: Richard Nixon tours the battlefield, 1969. One of the major issues in the 1968 US presidential election was America's future in Vietnam. Nixon's promises of troop withdrawals contributed significantly to his victory.

The United States committed every part of its non-nuclear arsenal to Southeast Asia, and arms manufacturers saw it as a testing ground for their latest technology: B-52s, helicopter gunships, heavy artillery, tanks, warships, chemical weapons, as well as over half a million men by 1968. Despite this onslaught, the US Army seemed unable to defeat the Communist guerrillas. The 1968 North Vietnamese Tet Offensive proved that American resources were stretched to the limit and the American public was becoming increasingly unhappy about a war that the most powerful nation on earth just couldn't win. In 1968, the bloodiest year of the war, 14,592 US troops were killed in action and over 90,000 wounded. The Johnson administration knew that the only way to end it was by negotiation and withdrawal and, on 31 March, President Johnson announced that bombing would ceasae north of the 20th parallel. This admission failed to salvage the 1968 presidential election for the Democrats, however, and in 1968 Republican Richard Nixon became president. Within months he announced the first troop withdrawals and plans for the Vietnamization of the ARVN, replacing US troops with Vietnamese. Nixon initiated a policy of negotiating with the North Vietnamese leadership, but he also secretly instituted the bombing campaign against Cambodia.

Nothing could make up for the hundreds of thousands of lives lost in the conflict. Over 50,000 Americans alone died, and the war cost over $100 billion.

Left: During the early 1960s the Vietnamese people were divided in their political allegiance. The suicide of this young Buddhist monk was a protest against the policies of the American-backed South Vietnamese government of Ngo Dinh Diem.

Right: Vo Nguyen Giap, the most skilled and successful of the North Vietnamese military leadership. An ardent Communist, his organization of the North Vietnamese guerrillas forced a long stalemate in the war against the South.

Far right: General Nguyen Cao Ky, commander of the South Vietnamese air force and one of the officers keenest to send bombers to North Vietnam.

Below: Shabby, but deadly Montagnard commandos, trained by US Special Forces advisers, use the Pleiyit Commando Training Center, 1963.

Below right: North Vietnamese leader Ho Chi Minh poses with a group of youthful supporters.

Above: A Marine HUS-1 helicopter supplies South Vietnamese troops in 1964. With a strength of 24 helicopters, the Marine transport squadron provided logistical support to ARVN forces from April 1962 until the first ground troops landed at Da Nang in March 1965.

Left: Robert McNamara (right) and General Lyman Lemnitzer (second right) visit US Military Assistant Command units, May 1962.

Right: A member of the 1st Special Forces Group guards a bunker at Jui Ba Den, the Vietnamese flag in the background, 1964.

Inset right: Constant vigilance was often not enough to prevent surprise attacks by Viet Cong guerrillas. Captain Donlon inspects the barbed wire perimeter of Nam Dang Special Forces camp which was attacked earlier in 1964.

Above right: By 1966, with many thousands of troops committed to the undeclared war in Vietnam, press briefings became a way of life for Robert McNamara.

Right: General Westmoreland inspects missile launchers in South Vietnam.

Above far right: US Army paratroops prepare to jump out over 'War Zone C' during Operation 'Junction City' in 1967. 'Junction City' involved one of the largest mass helicopter lifts ever, and the battle itself marked a watershed in the war. Afterwards the Viet Cong withdrew their main forces to Cambodia and Laos.

Far right: Men of H Co. 2nd Bn., 7th Marines pursue Viet Cong along a rice paddy, December 1965.

Left: Destruction and evacuation became all too common for many Vietnamese during the 1960s. US Marines evacuate villagers from an area infiltrated by Viet Cong, 1966.

Right: Veterans of the battle for Ia Drang valley move off, 1966.

Below left: US Special Forces continued training South Vietnamese in counter-insurgency techniques in Thailand during the mid-1960s, as part of America's long-term aim of 'Vietnamization' of the ARVN.

Below: The 'workhorse of the Vietnam war' – Huey (UH-ID helicopters) gunships on patrol, 1967.

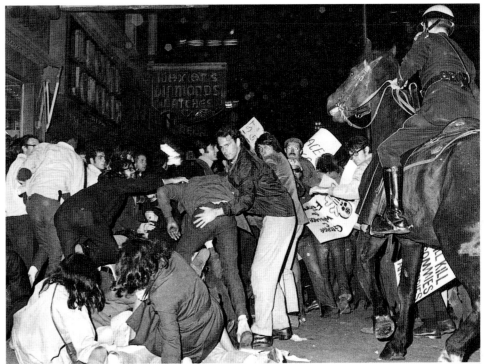

Left: A US Navy SEAL team disembarks from a heavily-armed boat in the Mekong Delta, 1967. By this time there were nearly half a million American servicemen in Vietnam, controlling an unprecedented quantity of firepower.

Above and right: The antiwar movement gathered momentum in 1967. No leading figure from the Johnson administration could travel anywhere in the world without encountering hostile protests. President Johnson was burned in effigy in Denmark (above left) and in the USA, the 1968 Democratic convention was dominated by antiwar protesters (above). The Republicans did not escape censure, either: George Wallace's campaign was interrupted by disturbances in New York, (right).

Above left: A US army gunner leads his team across a stream holding his M-60 high and dry over his shoulder.

Left: Marines conduct a house-by-house search for Viet Cong snipers at Ben Hoa, February 1968.

Above and right: After intense diplomatic pressure from the USA, Australia sent military advisers to Vietnam in 1964, and a consignment of troops the following year. Members of the 1st Australian Armoured Regiment receive a briefing in front of their Centurion tanks in 1968 (right). The Australian presence in Vietnam was extremely controversial and protests occurred in Sydney (above) as they did in other major cities around the world.

These pages: 1968 saw some of the most bitter fighting of the war as the North Vietnamese Army (NVA) launched the Tet Offensive and continued the siege of Khe Sanh. On the night of 30 January, while most of the South Vietnamese were celebrating new year, the Viet Cong and NVA soldiers launched surprise attacks in 100 major cities, even occupying part of the US embassy in Saigon for a short while. The counter-attack by American and ARVN forces was devastating and resulted in 30,000 enemy deaths. Although the North Vietnamese failed to dislodge the Americans, it was evident that American forces were not only fully stretched, but strangely vulnerable to the guerrilla forces who they outnumbered.

Above left: A Viet Cong jungle hideout is bombed by the USAAF.

Left: A well camouflaged US Navy SEAL moves cautiously through the thick jungle.

Above: A Long Range Patrol team opens fire against the enemy.

Right: A squad leader armed with an M-60 and plenty of ammo stares into the jungle. Despite almost unlimited resources, the USA did not have an adequate strategy for winning the war. By 1969 the call to end US involvement in Vietnam was almost unanimous, and after heavy American losses in the battle for Hamburger Hill in May, American ground troops were never committed to a major encounter with enemy forces again. From then on South Vietnamese troops, supported by American air power, bore the brunt of the fighting.

SOURIEZ
ÇA IRA MIEUX.

QUÉBEC
NOTRE. SEULE. PATRIE.

QUÉBEC. SAIT. FAIRE
L'INDÉPENDANCE.

LE. QUÉBEC. AUX. QUÉBÉCOIS.

A Decade of Protest

The image which the term 'the sixties' conjures up is primarily an optimistic one. Sixties' music, sixties' fashion, love-ins all bespeak color and vibrancy. But the radical changes in individual behavior and in society at large were hard won. Centuries of slowly evolving tradition were not to be overturned without a struggle. The processes that went into this struggle make the sixties, more than any other decade of the twentieth century, a decade of protest.

The rise of nationalist feeling, related in a complex way to the end of colonialism, was felt throughout the world in the sixties in southern and west Africa, in Algeria – even in French Canada. The backlash to this trend also manifested itself in protests such as the Organization Armée Secrète (OAS) which opposed Algerian independence from France. But some forms of protest transcended such national and political divisions.

One such movement, if movement it can be called in the diversity of its aims and methods, was the anti-nuclear movement. Nuclear arms were the single most prominent subject of protest in the early years of the decade, especially in Britain. Each Easter the Campaign for Nuclear Disarmament (CND) organized a march from Aldermaston Atomic Weapons' Research Establishment to Trafalgar Square in central London. In spite of attracting 100,000 to the 1961 march, CND failed to stop the escalation of the government's nuclear program. This prompted more extreme action by the Committee of 100 led by 89-year-old philosopher Bertrand Russell. Russell and other leaders of the Committee were convicted of incitement to civil disobedience after picketing the Ministry of Defence and Russell served his sentence in

Brixton Prison. CND had its equivalent organizations throughout the world, such as the American Committee for a Sane Nuclear Policy, but after the Cuban Missile Crisis the threat of imminent nuclear war receded. The quest for peace and to 'ban the bomb' remained a *sine qua non* for political progressives of all degrees of seriousness throughout the decade, but after 1964 the thrust of active peace campaigning was transferred to opposing the war in Vietnam.

Just as anti-nuclear campaigning in Britain had attracted prominent liberal intellectuals, so did the antiwar campaigners in the US. These included author Norman Mailer, poet Robert Lowell, and famous baby expert Dr Benjamin Spock. At first antiwar protest was restricted to a minority dominated by this élite and by individual acts of fanaticism such as Quaker Norman Morrison burning himself to death outside the Pentagon building. But soon antiwar feeling entered the consciousness of the nation, especially of the young. For many the war represented not resistance to Communist aggression but the imposition of First World will on a Third World nation in an indefensible display of post-colonial muscle-flexing. But it was the carnage of thousands upon thousands of civilian deaths that brought opposition into the establishment camp, culminating in the 1967 resignation of Defense Secretary Robert McNamara, one of the war's architects.

Antiwar protest was to be the focus of much of the student unrest which swept through the US and Europe in the later 1960s. But just as anti-nuclear protest had been divided by differences of theory and method, so it was with opposition to the war in Vietnam. Student protesters tended to go so far as to supoprt the Viet Cong and to identify their antiwar stance with radical politics generally and with the new youth life-style – smoking dope, rock music, sexual liberation and the deliberately offensive use of obscene language. Such attitudes alienated traditional American liberals and weakened the peace protest.

Student protest generally culminated in 1968, the year anything seemed possible. It occurred on campuses across the US, France, Germany, Britain, and beyond the Iron Curtain in Poland and Czechoslovakia. 1968 was the zenith of the anti-authoritarianism which had been growing up with the generation that were now students. It undermined such basic assumptions as the need to work and earn money, and the inevitability and desirability of submitting to authority's demands. Many clashes were violent and some, such as those at Kent State University in the US, resulted in student deaths. The most colorful and publicized protests were those which rocked Paris that year.

Even the Olympics did not escape. The games opened in Mexico in 1968 with a massacre of students who were protesting against the vast cost of the games. It is still unclear exactly how many hundreds were killed. American athletes Tommie Smith and John Carlos aroused more adverse publicity by giving the Black Power salute after winning medals in the 200m sprint. American public opinion was outraged, and their protest saw them banished from the US team.

In a decade of vociferous protest, 1968 stood out as an exceptional year. Much was achieved by the marches, rallies and sit-ins of the sixties, but the new world was still a distant speck on the horizon.

Previous pages: Nationalist aspirations spread to Canada in October 1969, when francophone Québecois demonstrated in Montreal.

Above left: Anti-Vietnam protest in France provided the opportunity for the Communist party to condemn imperialism wherever it occured.

Left: American university campuses became a focus for protest in 1968: this is the campus at Berkeley.

Right: Capitol police in Washington rip off the shirt of 'yippie' Abbie Hoffmann in the belief that it had been constructed from a US flag, considered by the authorities an act of desecration and decidedly 'Un-American'.

99

Left: New York, May 1960, a group of Civil Defense violators who refused to take cover during an air-raid drill, await fingerprinting at City Hall.

Below left: 18 February 1961: the Committee of 100 arranged a sit-down protest outside the Ministry of Defence in London. This was the beginning of a campaign of mass civil disobedience to protest against weapons of mass destruction, and the Polaris agreement in particular.

Right: The international face of nuclear protest is encapsulated in this image of two protesters on a peace march in Italy in September 1961. The lefthand sign commemorates the UN Secretary-General Dag Hammarskjöld who had recently died in a plane crash.

Below right: The most venerable of peace protesters, Bertrand Russell (also seen seated, left), in Denmark in 1960 to receive the humanitarian Sonning prize.

Above: A group of Fidel Castro's supporters protest outside the United Nations in New York in April 1961 at US policy toward Castro.

Above right: The New York Council of the National Committee for a Sane Nuclear Policy protests over the government's policy on nuclear shelters in February 1962.

Right: July 1962: A group of mothers and children gather near the United Nations' building in New York to protest against nuclear weapons' testing and the harmful effects of radiation.

Above left: Four armed police wrestle a peace demonstrator to the ground at Groton, Connecticut in August 1962. He had been protesting at the launch of the Polaris-missile submarine *Alexander Hamilton* at the General Dynamics Shipyard.

Above: After completing a 109-mile 'march for peace', members of the committee for a Sane Nuclear Policy mass behind a police barrier at the United Nations Plaza, New York, April 1961.

Right: Mrs Susan Ginzberg and her two-month old son, Lark, demonstrate with others in City Hall Park, New York, April 1961, against the city-wide civil defense drill.

Left: June 1962: Members of the Campaign for Nuclear Disarmament arrange a lie-down protest in London to represent projected deaths from leukemia caused by Soviet and US nuclear tests.

ATOMKRIEG NEIN

MOUVEMENT SUISSE DE LA PAIX · SCHWEIZERISCHE BEWEGUNG FÜR DEN FRIEDEN · MOVIMENTO SVIZZERO PER LA PACE

Left: Swiss demonstrators carry a placard proclaiming 'No Nuclear War' outside the US embassy in Copenhagen, in April 1962. The protest was against resumption by the US of nuclear test detonations on 25 April 1962.

Right: A lady-like protest from antiwar women awaiting the arrival of the First Lady, Mrs Johnson, in New York, 1967.

Below: April, 1963: protesters outside the General Dynamics Shipyard, Groton, Connecticut, picketing the launch of the Polaris-missile submarine, *Daniel Webster*.

Left: Frankfurt, March 1965: police struggle to hold back protesters demonstrating outside the US Consulate General's office against the war in Vietnam and the use of gas in the war.

Below left: Mexico City, 1968: US Olympic athletes Tommie Smith (center) and John Carlos (right) giving the Black Power salute after receiving gold and bronze medals respectively in the 200 meters. The outrage which greeted their gesture resulted in their being banned from the American team.

Below: General de Gaulle, France's president, is received in July 1967 in Quebec where he supported popular demands for an independent Quebec.

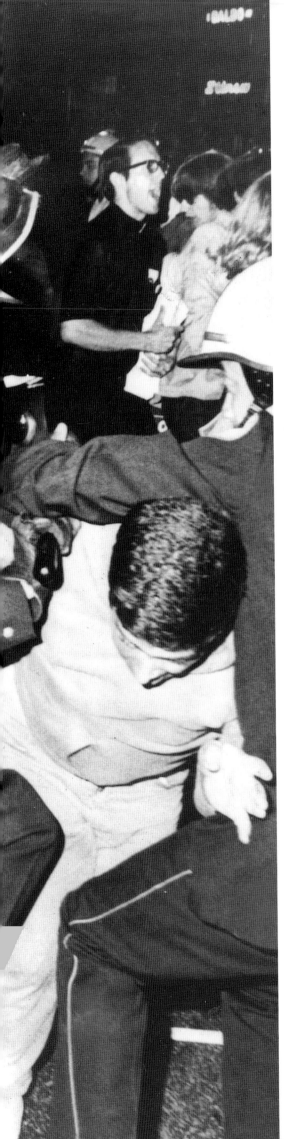

Left: October, 1968: Chicago police wield clubs, tear gas and the chemical mace to subdue thousands of antiwar protesters during the National Democratic Convention.

Above: Dr Benjamin Spock (fourth from right) leads antiwar demonstrators on a two-mile march from the Lincoln Memorial to the Pentagon at the beginning of a weekend peace vigil in October 1967.

Below: A student of the University of Wisconsin smiles down the barrel of a gun as National Guardsmen are called in to maintain order on the campus during a student strike, February 1969.

Above: Student protesters in Panama City, September 1966, demand the release of Luis Navas, a Communist student leader being held by the authorities on suspicion of murder. The students were dispersed by tear gas when they marched on the presidential palace.

Left: A demonstrator rises above a crowd of other protesters in Paris in May 1966. The demonstration, organized by several trades unions, followed a day-long strike aimed at highlighting the shortcomings of some government policies.

Above right: The peak of student protest in Paris came in May 1968 following week-long demonstrations by students demanding sweeping changes at the Sorbonne University. On the night of 11 May barricades of over-turned cars were erected in Rue Guy Lussac following a pitched battle between rioters and police which resulted in several hundred injuries.

Right: Mass protest in Paris, June 1968: protesters march with red and black flags.

Left: Student barricade erected in Paris's Latin Quarter on 11 June 1968, following the controversial drowning of a young demonstrator at Meulan on the outskirts of Paris.

Inset left: The counterblast to left-wing student protest is represented here by a member of the 'Occident Movement' burning a red flag on the boulevard des Italiens in Paris, May 1968.

Above: A Parisian student tries to protect his head from police truncheon blows during a demonstration protesting at the closing of the Sorbonne's Nanterre Annexe, May 1968.

Left: Antiwar protesters attempting to march from Grant Park to Convention Hall, Chicago, August 1968. National Guardsmen eventually resorted to using tear gas when the protesters broke through police lines.

Below: Rudi Dutschke, commonly known as 'Red Rudi', and chief ideologist of the German Socialist Students' Federation, pictured in 1968.

Right: Student demonstrators, some carrying a banner of Che Guevara, march along Reforma Boulevard in Mexico City to demand the dismissal of the chief of police.

Above: From left to right, Jerry Rubin, Abbie Hoffman, Thomas Hayden, Rennie Davis, Bobby Seale, Lee Weiner, John Froines and David Dellinger, the defendants in the 'Conspiracy 8' trial in 1969. The charge was conspiracy to riot, and the mixed aims of the defendants – yippies Rubin and Hoffman, Black Panther Seale and pacifist Dellinger – indicate the power of alliance in the politics of protest.

Right: London, 2 March 1969: school students and a few teachers took part in a demonstration in Hyde Park organized by the School Action Union. They presented a petition to the Department of Education and Science demanding, among other things, that the London Education Authority hand over control of schools to students and staff.

Below: Antiwar demonstrators, yippies and others clash with National Guardsmen in Grant Park, Chicago, 29 August 1968.

Time Out

'I can't get no satisfaction.'
'Scuse me while I kiss the sky.'
'All you need is love.'
Three lines from three great songs by three of the biggest names in rock music, each of which reflects one of the principal themes of the 1960s. You could say that the Rolling Stones, Jimi Hendrix and The Beatles have captured the essence of the decade: the initial frustration felt by young people, the escapism achieved through a diet of hallucinogenic drugs, the pursuit of psychedelic harmony.

But there was far more to it than that. The sixties saw an explosion in popular culture from which the world still hasn't recovered, and of which we are the inheritors.

Frustration certainly played a part in it. As the sixties dawned, so did the realization that, other than Elvis, few musicians had their fingers quite on the pulse of the increasingly disillusioned youth. Young people wanted something new, fresh and original. What they got was the Beatles.

Beatlemania conquered the world and opened the door of global success to many other bands. Bands like the Rolling Stones and the Who challenged traditional values and presented a more aggressive and anarchic face to the world. More subversive still were underground musicians like the Doors, the Grateful Dead, Velvet Underground, Pink Floyd

and the great Jimi Hendrix, whose songs broached all manner of taboo subjects, like sex, violence, guilt and death. Musical experimentation was in and no one was going to turn back the tide.

Perhaps more than anything else, the sixties were an era of vast cross-fertilization between cultural strands. Once an acoustic protest folk singer, Bob Dylan shocked the purists when he went electric, while on a larger scale music became intertwined with drugs, eastern mysticism, psychedelia, pop art and peace. Artists and writers mixed with rock stars, who went out with models and actresses, who hob-nobbed with the gentry, and set the gossip columns buzzing. Once the Beatles and other icons adopted certain drugs and sought the counsel of the oriental guru the Maharishi Mahesh Yogi, their fans were bound to imitate them. Other influential figures like Harvard academic Dr Timothy Leary and writer Ken Kesey were to promote the drug LSD as having enlightening properties, leading to self-discovery and spiritual fulfilment, and marijuana also did a brisk trade.

A separate musical scene, black music in the sixties merits a book in itself, but just a mention of some of the big names brings home the rich legacy of the decade: Diana Ross and the Supremes, Smokey Robinson, the prodigious Little Stevie Wonder, the Drifters, Marvin Gaye, Sam Cooke, Otis Red-

ding, James Brown, Aretha Franklin, and many more besides. By and large, these artists' lyrics addressed the burning issue of 'lurve' and rarely ventured into controversial topics like racial strife or poverty.

But then, musical success was not confined to the radical, to which the mellower Cliff Richard, Cilla Black, Lulu, the Dave Clark Five, Sandy Shaw, the Monkees and numerous others are testimony. Certainly, the mass media changed the face of popular culture in the sixties.

But TV played a more crucial role than simply that of publicizing rock stars. What appeared on TV in the sixties both reflected and fashioned the attitudes of the age. Satire took to the small screen, most notably in the irreverent *That Was The Week That Was*, and politicians became more exposed to public scrutiny in increasingly searching current affairs programs and chat shows. Drama and comedy became more realistic, the once prolific westerns gave way to more varied kinds of adventure series. *The Avengers, Dr Who, The Man from UNCLE, The Untouchables*, and *Star Trek*, are now the staple diet of any nostalgia boom. Realism was in, as exemplified by the British *Coronation Street* and one-off dramas like *Cathy Come Home* and *Up the Junction*, and new comedies took different forms: compare *Bewitched* with Rowan and Martin's quick-fire *Laugh-In*, for example.

However, TV remained firmly under the control of the establishment and, while it certainly became more liberal and offended conservatives like Mrs Mary Whitehouse, it was never part of the counter-culture which was symbolized by sex, drugs and rock'n'roll ... and, of course, the unforgettable Woodstock.

The same could be said of the sporting world, which carried on largely unaffected by the goings-on of Warhol, Ginsberg and their ilk. The sixties produced some of the biggest sporting celebrities ever known: Cassius Clay became world heavyweight boxing champion, a global superstar, and Muhammad Ali. Billie-Jean King (née Moffitt) was notching up the first of her 20 Wimbledon titles, while Rod Laver won two Grand Slams. Jack Nicklaus won two consecutive Masters titles, Willie Shoemaker rode his 5000th winner and England won the 1966 soccer World Cup, but Brazil possessed the brightest soccer star, Pelé. The USA and USSR did battle in the Rome, Tokyo and Mexico Olympics, and in the USA football gained the AFL, the Super Bowl and a new popularity.

But while sport grew in prominence in the public's consciousness, the sixties will be remembered more for the extraordinary eruption of popular culture, which blasted the world into the modern age.

Previous pages: The Beatles, as most people would like to remember them, in the earlier part of their careers.

Far left: The definitive 'Hi Honey, I'm home' show. Dick Van Dyke and his screen wife Mary Tyler Moore make light work of their suburban lives, even if current mores prevented them from sharing a double bed for the pillow talk scenes. That apart, *The Dick Van Dyke Show*'s popularity had a lot to do with its realism.

Left: Billie-Jean Moffitt (later Billie-Jean King) in action at Wimbledon in 1964. She went out to Australia's Margaret Smith, who in turn lost in the final to Maria Bueno. But of course, Wimbledon was to see a great deal more of Billie-Jean in years to come.

Right: The master in action. Jimi Hendrix giving another virtuoso performance, throbbing with energy, bursting with passion, a completely new kind of experience. Hendrix embodied the revolutionary nature of sixties style and music: colorful, unrestrained and, to more conservative tastes, positively anarchic.

Above: The Drifters, who by the sixties were almost veterans. They started out in 1953 and retained a huge following through their metamorphosis from a gospel-based sound to middle-of-the-road pop.

Left: British evergreen Cliff Richard with Norrie Paramor as he collects one of his first gold discs. Cliff's career and style had certain similarities with Elvis Presley's, using films as vehicles for popular rock'n'roll numbers, but his clean living ensured he lasted rather longer.

Top right: 'I heard it through the grapevine' – Marvin Gaye, a velvety voice with a far-from-velvety message: Gaye broke with Motown tradition to tackle social and racial issues in his lyrics.

Right: Adam Faith, another fresh-faced Brit who would outlast the decade. He presented the acceptable face of rock in the sixties.

Far right: Joan Baez, the voice of protest in the sixties, and far more than just a folk singer.

Left: Janet Leigh (left), Pete Seeger and Bobbie Gentry appearing on *The Smothers Brothers Comedy Hour*, which went out at prime time on Sunday evenings. Seeger was something of a survivor, being an old-school Communist who had withstood the McCarthyite purge of the fifties and the establishment's anti-Communist sensitivities during the Cold War.

Above: Bob Dylan and Joan Baez pose for cameras in London's Embankment Gardens during Dylan's spring tour in 1965. Their popularity stemmed largely from the sentiments which they articulated: an impatience with the authorities, a desire for harmony between peoples, all packaged in a simple folk idiom.

Left: The Beatles at the height of their powers in the mid-sixties. George and John listen while Paul and Ringo keep jamming.

Below: The Fab Four taking a breather from their busy schedule in February 1968. This was the year in which they released 'the white album,' a double album entitled simply *The Beatles*. Here was a testimony to the versatility of the band, with 30 songs covering a wide range of themes and styles. In their early days they would leave a song after two or three takes, happy with the result. For this album some songs took in the region of 200 takes.

Above: George, Paul, John and Ringo in about 1964. Brian Epstein, their manager, was responsible for dressing the Beatles in suits, which posed a difficult problem for those who wished to portray them as long-haired degenerates. For such as these, the last straw was when the boys received MBEs from the Queen at Buckingham Palace; some recipients of other honors even returned theirs in protest. The whole matter provides an interesting example of how the establishment wished to keep up with the momentous popular changes which seemed to be driving a wedge between the generations in the sixties.

Left: The Grateful Dead, just hanging out and looking mellow. In 1965 the band teamed up with the novelist Don Kesey and his 'Merry Pranksters', of magic bus fame. Together they staged 'Trips Festivals' or 'Acid Tests' on the Californian seaboard, which represented an all-out assault on the senses: strobes, light shows, multiple film projections, loud music, all washed down with a heady cocktail of Kool-Aid and LSD. Their lighting and sound engineer, Owsley, was reputed to manufacture the best LSD on the market.

Above: Older and wiser? The Grateful Dead pose outside another West Coast venue later on in their careers. It was no coincidence that they were at the forefront of the mid-sixties counter-culture, which had its origins in their home town of San Francisco. They were still around to wow the crowd at Woodstock in 1969.

Right: Jefferson Airplane played alongside the Grateful Dead at San Francisco's Fillmore Hall in 1965. They were a classic example of the fusion of American folk and the electric sounds brought over by the British bands. Airplane also put in an appearance at Woodstock.

Left: Paul Simon and Art Garfunkel, a duo whose calm voice of protest, clever lyrics and memorable tunes have ensured a following that has outlived their partnership, which began in the late fifties.

Bottom left: The less aggressive face of pop in the sixties: the Beach Boys. Where other groups preached disenchantment and rebellion, these Californian boys extolled the virtues of surf, sand and bronzed babes in some immortal songs.

Below: Lou Reed, linchpin of the Velvet Underground. Dissonant, cacophonous, relentless in its intensity, the Underground's music was some of the most subversive to be heard in the late sixties, with its accent on drugs, decadence and death. Andy Warhol used them in his multimedia extravaganza *The Exploding Plastic Inevitable* in 1965.

Right: The music establishment fights back: The Monkees were a manufactured group, restoring something of the conventional images which the responsible classes wished music to portray. In place of mass hysteria, drugs and rebellion, The Monkees provided a bit of harmless fun in the surf, with four good-looking lads singing boppy tunes. And they were a great success.

Left: The other side of sixties music. The Supremes were not in the business of protest or politics; affairs of the heart provided them with more than enough material with which to create a string of top ten hits on both sides of the Atlantic through most of the decade. They were Motown's flagship and now, long after their break-up, cover versions of their songs keep hitting the top.

Above: This young man was another talent spotted by Motown and nurtured to superstardom. Little Stevie Wonder was one of the great musical geniuses to find his feet in the sixties, combining technical virtuosity with an ear for a good tune. But he did not confine his efforts to catchy love ditties and ballads. One of his earlier recordings is of Bob Dylan's gloomy song *Blowing in the Wind.*

Left: The Who in 1964. From left to right, Peter Townshend, Roger Daltry, Keith Moon, John Entwistle. It was in 1965 that they sprang to fame, with *My Generation*, a UK hit which brought to the boil all the tensions of the youth of the day. Their defiant lyrics and roaring energy conveyed an aggressive attitude to their music.

Below left: The Animals, another group which arose out of the art college scene in sixties. This picture shows them in action on ITV's rock show *Ready Steady Go!*

Right: Ray Davies, another art college product, and The Kinks, who employed subtler methods of deriding authority than most. Wit and satire were integral to their act, and the songwriting skills of Davies gave them a unique place in sixties rock.

Below right: The immortal Cilla Black, who offered a slightly different sort of 'Mersey Sound.' Thirty years on she would be a TV megastar in Britain and the nation's second-favorite grandmother.

Below: Scotland's Lulu, one of the most popular solo artists in Britain in the sixties. With such lasting hits as *Shout!* she is another of the great evergreens.

Overleaf: The bad boys of rock: set up as the antithesis of the Beatles, the Rolling Stones were something else besides.

138

Above left: When Jimmy Page starts on a riff, you can't help but lose yourself in it, as Led Zeppelin's Robert Plant does here. Zeppelin popularized the heavy metal genre in the sixties.

Above: Eric Clapton, who rose to fame as guitarist with Cream, one of the most innovative bands of the sixties, which spawned a generation of heavy metal groups. Clapton set new standards of virtuosity in the rock world with his blinding guitar skill.

Left: 'All you need is love.' The Beatles in their 1967 liveries, leading the way in promoting hippy values.

Right: Bob Dylan, a one-man microcosm of musical development in the sixties in the US. He played a crucial part in the convergence of folk and protest, before adopting the electric sounds imported from Britain. He remains one of the legendary figures of the decade.

Left: The Doors (from left to right): Robbie Krieger, John Densmore, Ray Manzarek and Jim Morrison. This band was special, combining haunting, pulsating music and intelligent lyrics on subjects which the world had previously held as taboos: death, violence, sex and guilt.

Below left: Moon the Loon – The Who's drummer, Keith Moon, was as wild off-stage as on; he frequently ended his performance by destroying the drum-kit, having refined his technique on hotel rooms.

Below: The colorful plumage of the great Jimi Hendrix, seen here in 1968. Believe it or not, Hendrix signed up in 1967 as the support act for The Monkees, such was his inability to say no to anything.

Right: Janis Joplin, another tragic victim of the excesses which marred the music scene in the sixties. Her passionate, physical style of blues made her one of the great legends of the age.

Far left: Yabadabadoo! Out for a spin around their stone-age suburbia, the Flintstones reinforced the social values which so much of the sixties culture seemed to threaten.

Left: Roger Moore, warming up for his stint as James Bond, in *The Saint*, a long-running and popular series which first hit the small screen in 1962.

Below left: 'To boldly go where no man has gone before.' NBC made 78 *Star Trek* episodes, little imagining that the program would attain a cult following and spawn a series of blockbuster movies 25 years later. All but the blonde lieutenant in this photo have remained as the nucleus of *Star Trek*'s Hollywood success, albeit with a few more wrinkles.

Right: 'Say goodnight, Dick.' 'Goodnight, Dick!' Rowan and Martin's *Laugh-In* provided a clever mixture of conventional presentation with quick-fire off-beat humor, which appealed to a range of tastes in America. It started in 1967 and quickly became the most popular show in the US, attracting various guests, including Richard Nixon.

Below: Patrick McGoohan canvasses votes in Portmeirion in an episode of the ever-popular and enigmatic *The Prisoner*.

Below right: 'Good thinking, Batman.' Caped crusader and sidekick Robin, the Boy Wonder, in a tense moment before inevitably saving the world from the forces of evil.

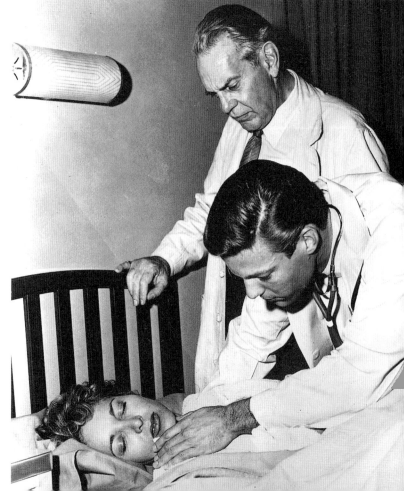

Left: The exploits of the security services earlier in the decade were the catalyst for the proliferation of spy series such as *The Man from UNCLE*, an acronym-riddled American product, which set the humorous tone for future efforts.

Far left below: Hogan's Heroes still employed the monocled Nazi officer as the archetypal baddy.

Below left: Richard Chamberlain's bedside manner won *Dr Kildare* a large following during the sixties.

Right: The Donna Reed Show was a popular sitcom which ran on ABC from 1958 to 1966, a far cry from the anarchic style of the *Laugh-In*.

Below: David Frost, anchorman of *That Was The Week That Was*, the BBC's revolutionary satirical series, which first went out in November 1962.

Below right: Patrick McGoohan takes the title role in *Secret Agent*, another spy story made in England.

Learn the great American sport of Wide-Tracking in a great American sports car.

Wide-Tracking isn't hard to catch onto, once you've got the right equipment. And five of the most magnificent pieces of equipment around this year, are those bearing the Pontiac Firebird emblem. All five models sport such new excellences as smoother riding rear suspension, upper-level ventilation system (eliminating the need for vent windows) and new stuff under the hood. But, if you think Wide-Tracking is just a rich man's sport, you'll learn a thing or two by taking a look at some of our magnificently demure price tags. You can choose anything from a 175-hp Firebird to a 330-hp Firebird 400, each with a bevy of new safety equipment (like padded armrests, front and rear side marker lights) that makes Wide-Tracking more secure than ever. Front-wheel disc brakes, 4-speed shift, mag-style wheels and stereo tape are among the decisions *you'll* have to make. But the first thing you'll have to learn is which one of the Magnificent Five Firebirds is for you. Drive one . . . it's a very educational experience.

The Magnificent Five are: Firebird, Firebird Sprint, Firebird 350, Firebird H.O. and Firebird 400 (shown).   Pontiac Motor Division

GM
MARK OF EXCELLENCE

Wide-Track **1968** Pontiacs

Left: An advertisement for the 1968 range of Wide-Track Pontiac Firebirds, flagship of the General Motors fleet. The targeting of this advert is self-evident: clean-cut college kids, who wouldn't dream of rioting to the lyrics of Jim Morrison.

Below: As a disillusioned world longed for a little excitement in their lives, the wealthier members of a society were encouraged to find it in faster cars, like this handsome Aston Martin DB5 Convertible. James Bond gave Aston Martins enhanced credibility as glamour-cars, although Sean Connery had the benefit of optional rocket-launchers, armor-plating and bullet-shields.

Right: Definitely a machine for cruising down the highways on the West Coast of America with the Beach Boys blaring from the radio. This Volkswagen Buggy illustrates the specialization which manufacturers were prepared to indulge in to tap the prevailing mood of the times.

Below right: America's one true purpose-built sportscar, the Corvette. This beautifully sleek and powerful machine had quite a different line from its stylish forebears of the fifties.

Above left: Beat poet Allen Ginsberg, extolling the virtues of marijuana in a chilly Greenwich Village in November 1965, publicity which gave the drugs culture an extra impetus.

Above: Former Harvard lecturer, Dr Timothy Leary, advocated the use of hallucinogenic drugs as a means of expanding one's consciousness, founding the League for Spiritual Discovery, which quite by chance bore the same initials as the drug which he championed: LSD.

Left: Maharishi Mahesh Yogi, Indian guru to, amongst others, the Beatles. He became a major figure in the confluence of drugs, eastern mysticism, psychedelia and rock music which characterized the late sixties.

Right: A tragically early death in the sixties was that of Marilyn Monroe. By 1961, when this still was taken on the set for *The Misfits* (with Clark Gable), Marilyn's health was already in decline. She died the following year.

Above left: André Previn and Mia Farrow, Tiny Tim and Vici Buddinger, party-goers in an age when the cult of the media celebrity really took off. Anyone who was anyone entered the popular consciousness, even for simply attending a big party.

Above: Wilhelm Reich, whose writings on sexual liberation, youth frustration and rebellion sought to legitimize the movements labeled 'subversive' by the establishment.

Left: The sultry pout of Brigitte Bardot, sex goddess, who had established herself in a film career since the early fifties. She may not be remembered as a great actress, but she certainly epitomized the mood of the era when she remarked: 'I wish I had invented sex. Sex is number one.'

Right: Jane Fonda, better known in the *Barbarella* days for her looks, rather than her politics, strikes a provocative pose in 1967. The film which made her famous was a raunchy science-fiction romp which did not conform to the modesty of earlier cinematic mores.

Top left: The Green Bay Packers getting the better of the Kansas City Chiefs, whom they beat 35-10 in the 1967 Super Bowl at the Memorial Coliseum, Los Angeles.

Left: The New York Jets (in white) going down expectedly to the Baltimore Colts in their NFL Championship year in the 1969 Super Bowl in Miami. They lost 16-7.

Above: Roger Maris hits his record-breaking 61st home run of the season in 1961, to beat Babe Ruth's 1927 record. Purists may have been disappointed to see the Babe's record fall to a player who could not match him for all-round stature in the game, but New York Yankee supporters were bound to feel proud that it was one of their boys who had done it again.

Right: Arnold Palmer happily passes on the green jacket to his young sparring partner Jack Nicklaus, who in 1965 won his second Masters at Augusta, setting a new tournament record of 271.

Above far left: America's Arthur Ashe, who went out to the mighty Rod Laver in the semi-finals at Wimbledon in 1968. He won the tournament in 1975.

Above left: A familiar sight: Billie-Jean King (née Moffitt) on one of the earlier of the 20 occasions on which she held up a Wimbledon trophy. Like Ashe, she went on to win in 1975.

Left: The first win for a professional at Wimbledon, and Rod Laver's third victory in the tournament, this one against fellow Australian Tony Roche in straight sets in 1968.

Above: 'Sting like a bee.' Sonny Liston wouldn't disagree with that, having been knocked out in the first minute of his bout with Cassius Clay in 1965, which gave Clay the world heavyweight title.

Right: At the other end of the decade (1961) Floyd Patterson was heavyweight boxing champion.

'There are people on the pitch. They think it's all over . . . it is now!' The TV commentator's words as the final whistle went in the 1966 soccer World Cup Final have become part of England's sporting folklore. England beat West Germany 4-2 in a thriller of a match, which was not without its controversy.

Left: West Germany (further from camera) and England line up for the national anthems before the match at London's Wembley Stadium. Geoff Hurst (third from right) scored a hat-trick of goals, the second of which caused a storm of protest from the West Germans, who questioned whether the ball had actually crossed the line. In the event, it gave England the breakthrough they needed, and Hurst's third goal sealed their victory.

Below left: With only 30 seconds to go in the World Cup Final, West Germany's Wolfgang Weber slots one past the England goalkeeper, Gordon Banks, to wreck home supporters' premature celebrations and force extra time. England's manager, Alf Ramsey, marched out on to the turf during the break and hissed at his team: 'You've beaten them once. No go out and do it again.' As every British schoolboy knows, this is exactly what they went out and did.

Right: A valuable collector's item: the program for the World Cup Final of 1966.

Below: England's captain, Bobby Moore, happily receives the Jules Rimet World Cup from Her Majesty the Queen after his team's exhausting battle at Wembley. The trophy itself had earlier been stolen from its temporary home, but was found in time for the big match . . . by a dog. The match had started with an early German lead through Helmut Haller, but Martin Peters brought England back into the game . . . and the rest, as they say, is sporting history.

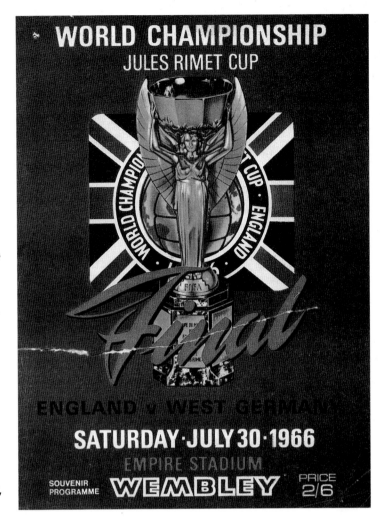

The Swinging 60s

The phrase 'Swinging Sixties' conjures up an irresistible vision of long-legged, mini-skirted lovelies, of gentle, flower-bedecked hippies, of a great fancy-dress party at which everyone got happily stoned. In the first half of the decade Britain burst out of the gray, careful fifties and became a world leader in fashion as well as pop culture. The first unmistakably sixties designer was Mary Quant, whose bold black-and-white designs swept first the British and then the American market in the early 1960s.

By this time the sixties scene was in full swing. With the explosion of music from Merseyside came a multiplication of styles and a new youth consciousness that sought to create its own distinct identity, while youth-oriented television shows on both sides of the Atlantic guaranteed the instant spread of new trends. The Beatles' abandonment of scruffy jeans in favor of collarless jackets, elastic-sided boots and the characteristic haircut was a milestone. Hair became a significant fashion statement, and the young Vidal Sassoon snipped his way to fame. Young men began to dress as flamboyantly as their girlfriends, and designer John Stephens' shop in Carnaby Street became the prototype for new-style fashion boutiques catering for men as well as women.

As hair grew longer, skirts grew shorter, and the mini-skirt became a symbol of all that Swinging London represented: youth, fun, style and sex. In fall 1964 the Paris couturier André Courrèges gave the fashion world's seal of approval to sixties style by showing mini-skirts in his collection, and the following year Saint Laurent took up the Op Art theme with his visually mesmerizing black-and-white dresses.

By the mid-1960s the clear visual differentiation between the sexes had broken down. While women could cultivate an androgynous look, with short hair, trousers and flat shoes, and the reedlike Twiggy was the ideal model, men grew their hair and adopted an altogether more relaxed and sensuous body language. In the US the strong folk tradition had survived the onset of pop and became a significant factor in an increasingly in-turned, non-materialistic, drug-oriented youth culture. What started as a minor cult in San Francisco turned into the 1967 summer of love, as a new wave of psychedelia and hippy counter-culture spread worldwide from California. Beads, kaftans, cheesecloth shirts, Afghan coats and, of course, cannabis became the order of the day. Designers soon caught on to the prevailing mood, with the eighteenth-century dandy look – satin or crushed velvet trousers and ruffled shirt; the piratical look – knickerbockers and waistcoats; and the ethnic look – Zandra Rhodes' billowing dresses with batwing sleeves in swirling prints. As well as the mini-skirt, now worn with soft leather thigh boots, the midi and even the maxi became fashionable, and for the first time in fifty years women walked the daytime city streets in skirts that swept the ground. The sixties style revolution had come full circle.

Previous page: Flowers and beads at the New York night club 'The Electric Circus.'

Left and above: Sixties fashion style varied from the hipster mini-skirt to casual evening wear in psychedelic prints.

Right: Andy Warhol, sixties icon, and protegées.

Left: Comic Lenny Bruce is searched by a policeman after his arrest on 4 October 1961, for allegedly using obscene language during his act at a San Francisco nightclub. American laws banned lewd exhibition and obscene language in public places, reflecting a still repressive attitude to both public and private behavior.

Below left: New York police try to enforce a law forbidding song festivals in and around Central Park. Here a cheerful group of Greenwich Villagers, sun roof down to accommodate their instruments, awaits the release of those arrested during a minor riot in Washington Square in April 1961.

Right: Britain was the prime mover on the fashion scene; youthful strollers on New York's Fifth Avenue, in their sober slacks and reefer jackets, are fascinated by British model Lorra McDonough in her plastic mini-skirt, matching battle jacket and white boots.

Below: The widowed Jacqueline Kennedy, having revolutionized the White House scene during the Camelot Years, remained a style icon throughout the sixties, finally marrying millionaire Greek shipowner Aristotle Onassis in 1968.

Below right: The singing, swinging mood spread rapidly; here a group of Italian youths stage an impromptu song session in the ruins of the Forum in Rome.

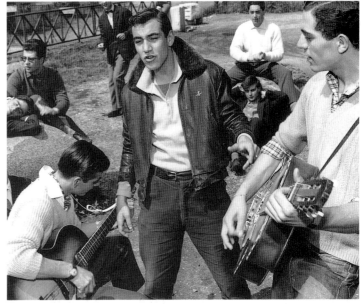

Far left: Film star Rita Tushingham, who made her name in the cult movie *The Knack*, arrives at the gala ball after the world premiere of *Dr Zhivago*, wearing a futuristic Op Art dress inspired by the Parisian couturier Courrèges.

Left: Actress Julie Christie electrified the film world with her portrayal of an ambitious, amoral young woman in the stylish and influential *Darling* in 1965, for which she won an Oscar. She is here seen meeting the US press.

Below left: A holiday family is caught in a teenage stampede on Hastings beach on the south coast of England. The summer of 1964 was enlivened by clashes between rival gangs of Mods and Rockers in various coastal resorts. Mods were smartly dressed and rode scooters, Rockers were tough and casual and rode motor bikes.

Right: Some of the *Ciao Manhattan* cast and crew prepare to shoot a scene in a New York health club in 1967. By now the underground film industry of the earlier years has joined the mainstream in the increasingly open and liberal atmosphere.

Below: Youth protest takes many forms; this group of singing clapping teenagers have taken refuge from police in a Sunset Strip coffee bar.

Far left: San Francisco was the origin and focus of the hippy movement.

Left: Cathy McGowan, presenter of the British pop television show *Ready Steady Go!*, became a fashion icon with her smooth flowing hair, pale lipstick and crocheted beret.

Below left: Anything goes in sixties nightclubs, including his-and-hers fur. Much ingenuity and home dressmaking skill went into the creation of far-out gear before it became available from stores.

Right: The hippy world, with its emphasis on a self-contained lifestyle and individual self-development, was at first treated by the media as a youthful aberration. By 1967, however, the hippies and their ways warranted front-page treatment.

Below: Valerie Solanas under arrest in June 1968 for the attempted murder of Andy Warhol. Solanas was the author of a manifesto advocating the extermination of the male sex in the interests of world peace. She was adopted as a heroine by the more extreme wing of the growing women's movement.

Newsweek
OCTOBER 30, 1967
TROUBLE IN HIPPIELAND

Left: Andy Warhol with acolytes. An archetypal sixties figure in the art and media world, he moved on from underground film in 1966 and launched his *Exploding Plastic Inevitable* mixed-media show, with deafening music, films and slides, colored lights and strobes.

Below left: By the mid-sixties the drop-out, Pop Art scene had spread as far as Manila in the Philippines.

Below: Warhol and his assistant Mr Melanga apply silkscreen paint to the paper dress worn by Nico of the pop group Velvet Underground, had been discovered and promoted by Warhol. Throw-away clothes had a vogue on the fashion scene, and this paper dress retailed at just two dollars.

Right: Sixties chick weds king of swing: Mia Farrow, young star of the television series *Peyton Place*, married Frank Sinatra, who was twice her age, in November 1966 and is seen here attending a masked ball thrown by best-selling author Truman Capote.

Left: The hippy culture, with its espousal of peace, love, eastern mysticism and communal living, soon spawned its own shops, providing all the paraphernalia of pop-Buddhism – temple bells, beads and joss sticks. This hippy store opened in the Boulevard St Michel in Paris in November 1967.

Above: In Cologne, West Germany, the demand is for fashion boutiques rather than prayer wheels. Modeled on London's Carnaby Street, this boutique in a department store supplies lurex tights and mini-skirts to the with-it West German young.

Right: At a hippy happening in Los Angeles, nature's child has created a leafy crown for himself.

Left and above left: The first large open-air hippy gatherings were held in Golden Gate Park, San Francisco, and Tompkins Park, New York. The hippies' commitment to their chosen lifestyle varied widely; only a small proportion of the huge crowds that gathered at any open-air Flower Power event had wholly severed their links with social convention.

Above: Drugs were an essential ingredient of the hippy scene. Marijuana was widely available, but LSD remained a minority pursuit after it was hastily outlawed in 1966. These hippies are staging an all-night vigil as they await the release of one of their number charged with selling LSD to a minor.

Right: In New York's Central Park in March 1967, thousands gather for an 'expression of love for all mankind.'

Above: The grounds of Woburn Abbey, English stately home and seat of the Duke of Bedford, look much the worse for wear after a three-day love-in.

Left: Home is a doorway for this happy pair in the rundown Haight Ashbury district of San Francisco, where in the early 1960s beatnik bohemianism and Acid crystalized into a widely publicized lifestyle available to anyone prepared to leave home and drift West. Flower Power began here.

Above right: Dallas's 'In Crowd' nightclub is an avalanche of color and music.

Below right: A 'be-in' on Boston Common, 'just for the joy of it', ends with linked hands in the chilly waters of the Frog Pond.

Left: Carnaby Street in London's West End and the King's Road in Chelsea became the high fashion spots of the decade, packed with young, trendy boutiques like Biba and Lord John. Of the two fashionable looks, the boyish sporty style meant T-shirt dress or mini-skirt, colored or patterned tights, and long boots or flat shoes. Hair was cropped and sculpted into an updated version of the twenties bob; Vidal Sassoon made his name with his skilful and sympathetic cutting. An impishly irreverent nostalgia for the heyday of imperialism inspired Union Jack waistcoats, hats and knickers.

Above: Carnaby Street in 1967, looking surprisingly unexciting on a gray Saturday afternoon.

Right: The teenage fashion model Twiggy, with her huge kohl-rimmed eyes and waif-like figure, here epitomizes the dolly-bird look, in a sweet gingham dress tied with flouncy bows. Skinny-rib sweaters and crocheted tops were also essential features of this alternative fashion style.

Above left: This couple find a peaceful spot on top of a psychedelic van at the three-day love-in at Woburn Abbey.

Below left: Although Carnaby Street was the true fashion mecca of London's young, the King's Road was the place to see and be seen. When coffee bars were full the kerb would do fine.

Above: One lasting legacy of the hippy movement was an awareness of the benefit of relaxation. 'White collar' hippies like these cultivated body awareness and emotional release without the use of narcotics, learning physical relaxation in order to tune into their feelings and to heighten their appreciation of the environment.

Right: Peace, love, and music in New York's Tompkins Square.

Left: Some alternative groups developed elaborate ceremonies to mark the rituals of the movement. Each new candidate had to be baptized by the 'priests' of the community, to cleanse them from the sin of violence and war. Hippy weddings in many ways followed conventional ones, with a priest officiating, and a best man and a maid of honor, as shown here. A marriage license was issued but was valid only for three months, renewable if the couple wished.

Below left: Yippies (Youth International Party) had a somewhat more political flavor than hippies, particularly in their association with the anti-Vietnam peace movement. Founded in 1967 by New Left radicals Jerry Rubin and Abbie Hoffmann, the Yippies developed out of the more radical end of the peace movement. Here they gather in Central Park to celebrate Easter with a yip-out.

Right: A British couple bring their children to a love-in.

Below: A sing-along at Detroit's first love-in at Belle Isle Park.

Scenes from hippy happenings. As Flower Power spread to a mass market, the original styles and concepts became much diluted. The record that epitomized the West Coast scene for the rest of the world was not the Grateful Dead's first album, but Scott Mackenzie's crowd-pleasing ballad 'If You're Going to San Francisco (Wear Some Flowers in Your Hair)', while the musical *Hair* showed just how marketable the hippy image could be as long as the music was commercial and the element of revolt transformed into a voyeuristic spectacle.

Above: Yippies Jack Lebowitz and Bob Bower decked out in Easter bonnets for a yip-out in New York's Central Park: a peaceful gathering dedicated to 'the resurrection of the free.'

Left: Hippy gatherings and love-ins became indissolubly linked with protests against Vietnam and the draft. This long-haired young man stripped off and leapt into the fountain in the San Francisco Civic Center Plaza as a crowd of 12,500 peace marchers converged on City Hall.

Right: A harem-style yippie brandishing a toy gun forms one of a small crowd of protesters outside the building in which a House Un-American Activities subcommittee investigates disturbances at the Democratic National Convention in Chicago in 1968.

Left: Woodstock, in August 1969, was the music festival to end all festivals. 400,000 people turned up to hear names such as Jimi Hendrix, Janis Joplin, Joan Baez, The Who, Jefferson Airplane and the Grateful Dead. The extraordinary thing about Woodstock was that, despite the huge crowd and the large amount of marijuana and other drugs in circulation, there was no trouble. Other rock festivals at Denver, Palm Springs, and Los Angeles fared less well.

Below: Guests circle a newly married couple in a wedding dance after a hippy wedding in a park adjoining Berkeley City Hall.

Right: Hippies Italian-style on the Spanish Steps in Rome. By 1969, when this picture was taken, the police had lost patience and 57 people with no visible means of support were ordered out of Italy.

Below right: A vast free concert in London's Hyde Park given by the Rolling Stones on 5 July 1969 – their first live performance in fifteen months – becomes a requiem for guitarist Brian Jones, who had drowned in the swimming pool of his London home two days before.

Left: Sixties faces: Christine Keeler (left), who soared to notoriety in the Profumo scandal in 1963, is seen here six years later at a party to launch a new book on the Swinging Sixties, with photographer David Bailey, model Penelope Tree and singer Marianne Faithfull.

Below left: A delightfully ironic style comment at the end of the decade: while the older generation has succumbed (perhaps foolishly) to the rage for shorter skirts, the young have gone into midi and maxi styles.

Below: The New Breed, a New York boutique, offers Afro-American styles as fashion goes increasingly ethnic.

Right: Doss down where you are, is the hippy philosophy, here applied in the welcoming streets of Amsterdam.

Left: A perennial sixties image, as a youthful pot smoker draws on a half-smoked joint. The pressure to legalize cannabis became very strong in the late 1960s, in both the US and the UK, but the authorities found the anti-drug laws a useful tool for locking up high-profile anti-establishment figures.

Right: The giant five-day rock festival at Freshwater, Isle of Wight, England.

Below: By the end of the decade the hippy espousal of ethnic clothes had permeated the high-fashion scene. This elaborate dress, modeled by Penelope Tree, is based on American Indian styles and features a fur trim and lining, and a profusion of feathers.

Art goes Pop

The upheavals in society that characterized the sixties had their equivalents in the arts. Film, the visual arts, and literature not only reflected the reappraisals of traditional values, but also seemed at times under threat as new artforms emerged to supplant them. The growth of television in particular eroded cinema audience figures and suggested filmmaking might be a dying art form. A similar sentence was pronounced by some pundits on the novel, painting in oil and sculpture in stone, with the increasing incidence of assemblage, happenings, and performance art.

Reports of the death of art were, of course, exaggerated. Just as for all there were ructions in society, they did not spell the sudden death of traditional values and social mores, so, many artforms which had evolved over centuries, far from dying, took on a new lease of life. A fitting start to the decade, and emblematic of the shape of things to come, was the publication in the UK and United States of D H Lawrence's *Lady Chatterly's Lover*. In spite of the sexual explicitness of some of the book, a British court had found it 'Not Guilty' of obscenity in 1960.

The work of established authors developed during the decade. Samuel Beckett's bleak texts became sparer and more fragmentary as the decade progressed, and William Burroughs did his best to revolutionize the novel form by inventing the 'cut up' technique which combined words and sentences at random. But the more conventional American prose-writing scene remained ebullient, with novelists Saul Bellow, Ken Kesey, John Updike, Philip Roth, Vladimir Nabokov, Gore Vidal, and James Baldwin all in action. Truman Capote invented 'faction' in his novel *In Cold Blood* based on a true murder story, and Norman Mailer, Tom Wolfe and Hunter S Thompson elevated an overheated reportage to impressive heights of eloquence. Elsewhere in the world Solzhenitsyn was proving that the conventional novel could still have political impact in a repressive state; and Günter Grass and Gabriel García Marquez established a new tradition of 'magical realism.'

Meanwhile, the movie industry was changing in response to a shift in its audience. Throughout the sixties the mainstream public had been deserting movie theaters, preferring to watch television at home. The audiences left in the cinemas were predominantly under-30 and often relatively sophisticated. Films were now most likely to succeed by expressing at least mildly radical attitudes and exploring themes of sex or violence not permissible on TV. The biggest commercial hit in this new trend was Mike Nichol's *The Graduate*, a gently subversive look at sex roles and the 'generation gap' in suburban America, with a soundtrack by the popular young duo of Paul Simon and Art Garfunkel, and unknown actor Dustin Hoffman as the gauche male lead.

Previous pages: Marcello Mastroianni and Anita Ekberg in Federico Fellini's *La Dolce Vita*, a film whose specious social critique served to stimulate the imaginations of public and filmmakers alike.

Left: The three winners of the 1960 National Book Awards were, left to right, Philip Roth, the youngest-ever winner of an award at 27 for *Goodbye Columbus*; Richard Ellman for his biography *James Joyce*; and Robert Lowell for his poetry *Life Studies*.

Above right: Artist Christo has specialized in work involving the packaging or reinvention of existing objects. Here he wrapped the America House in Heidelberg in plastic sheeting as part of the Intermedia 69 exhibition there in May 1969.

Right: Alfred Hitchcock's 1960 film *Psycho* was a low-budget shocker that has achieved cult status over the years. The blood in the famous shower scene was, allegedly, chocolate sauce.

Arthur Penn's *Bonnie and Clyde*, also made in 1967, confronted an unjust society with a pair of childlike rebels, doomed to a climax of ultraviolent death at the hands of overserious adults.

The visual arts were dominated by Pop Art. Artists such as Andy Warhol and Roy Lichtenstein used mass-produced imagery such as coke bottles, brillo-pad boxes or cartoon strips and elevated them to the status of 'high art' by presenting them on a huge scale in art galleries. Warhol's rejection of the importance of the role of the artist (he preferred his assistants to produce his works) had something in common in principle if not in form, with the Minimalist art of Sol LeWitt and Donald Judd. They used industrial manufacturing techniques and the simple elemental shapes were often created by industrial craftsmen to the artists' designs. Related also to Pop was the *Art Informel* of such artists as Christo, who wrapped huge objects such as houses in plastic, or César, who presented man-made objects transformed by a breaker's-yard crusher into something else – art.

One of the great social changes which affected especially literary art was feminism. A landmark was the 1963 publication of Betty Friedan's *The Feminine Mystique*, a wholesale attack against the myth of the American wife and mother embodying special values which apparently justified second-class citizenship; Friedan's work included the 1966 foundation of the National Organization of Women, one reflection of the increasing number of women able to go to university and out to work.

Above left: Karel Reisz's 1960 film *Saturday Night and Sunday Morning* heralded a new standard of realism and provoked a strong reaction for the way it treated the main character's dissatisfaction with life and his affair with a married woman.

Left: From Russia with Love was the second of the hugely successful James Bond movies. Many consider this 1963 film to be the best Bond movie, with a fast but not completely implausible plot and not too many gadgets.

Above: Peter O'Toole as T E Lawrence and Anthony Quinn as Auda Abu Tayi in David Lean's four-hour epic of 1963 *Lawrence of Arabia*. The film set new standards for visual beauty for an epic film, although the characterizations were hardly profound. Albert Finney turned down the Lawrence role before it was offered to Peter O'Toole.

Right: Peter Sellers in one of the three roles he played in *Dr. Strangelove*, the manic anti-war comedy directed by Stanley Kubrick in 1963.

Left: Ursula Andress, the first Bond girl, rises from the sea in *Dr No*, 1962.

Above: Ingrid Bergman swaps her rich lover for a young law student in the 1961 film *Goodbye Again*.

Above right: Tom Courtenay spins a fantasy world for Julie Christie in the 1963 *Billy Liar*. Later turned into a musical, Billy Liar became a hugely popular figure, a Walter Mitty for the 1960s.

Right: Brilliantly evocative of swinging London, *The Knack*, 1965, combined visual gags and sexual frankness in a jaunty *Hard Day's Night* style.

Left: A heartening story of escape from the Nazis and a selection of catchy tunes have made *The Sound of Music*, 1965, the most popular film musical of all time.

Below left: Richard Burton as Mark Antony and Elizabeth Taylor as Cleopatra in the 1963 epic *Cleopatra*. The film was most notable for its great expense and length, but it brought together Taylor and Burton for the first time, and with spectacular results.

Right: The Beatles filming *A Hard Day's Night* in 1964. With new songs and a fast plot, the movie was a huge success.

Below: The musical version of Shaw's *Pygmalion, My Fair Lady*, 1964, pitted Audrey Hepburn's aspiring lady against Rex Harrison's arrogant elocutionist.

Above, above right, and right: Three films which owed their considerable popularity to their portrayal of swinging life: *Alfie* (1966), *Blow Up* (1965), and *Darling* (1965).

Left: Although extremely violent, *Bonnie and Clyde* (1967) with Faye Dunaway and Warren Beatty contrived to be a classy and pacey film through its masterly cinematography.

Left: Mia Farrow befriends some diabolists and finds herself pregnant by the devil in that seminal gothic melodrama, *Rosemary's Baby* (1968), a precurser to *The Exorcist*.

Right: Paul Newman is a convict in a chain gang in the 1967 *Cool Hand Luke*; eventually he is shot during an escape.

Below right: The archetypal sci-fi movie *2001: A Space Odyssey*, has attracted a widespread cult following but mixed critical acclaim through its portentousness and stunning visuals.

Above left: Campy space-romp of 1967, *Barbarella*, with Jane Fonda, was a classic piece of 1960s euro-fluff.

Left: The 1968 press launch for the Beatles' psychedelic cartoon, *Yellow Submarine*. Ringo and George appear here with 'Blue Meanie'.

Above right: The ultimate 1960s' road movie as two hairy-hippy drop-outs, Peter Fonda and Dennis Hopper, burn across America in *Easy Rider* (1969).

Right: Butch Cassidy and the Sundance Kid (1969) was an amusing and visually poetic tale of two lovable-rogue train robbers (Paul Newman and Robert Redford), which introduced the song 'Raindrops Keep Falling on my Head' to the world.

Far right: Texan cowboy (Jon Voight) comes to New York city to offer his services as a stud to wealthy women. He ends up looking after tubercular conman (Dustin Hoffman) in 1969 *Midnight Cowboy*.

Above, far left: The most prominent and enduring of feminist writers, Germaine Greer. In the 1960s she was known principally as a member of an Australian intellectual coterie in London which published *Oz* magazine.

Above left: Betty Friedan was, in many ways, the pioneer 1960s feminist, publishing her book *The Feminine Mystique* in 1963.

Above: The ultimate cliché image of women's liberation: in this case it is bra-discarding, rather than bra-burning. The three pictured here in Chicago, 1969, were charged with 'polluting the river' after tossing their bras into the water.

Left and right: Demonstrators picket the Miss America contest in Atlantic City, New Jersey, September 1969.

These pages: The 1960s was the era when the brave new world of modern architecture was at its most confident and aggressive.

Above left: Paul Rudolph's 1963 Art and Architecture building at Yale University.

Above: Louis Kahn's 1959-65 Salk Institute at La Jolla, California.

Right: Le Corbusier's 1960 Carpenter Center at Harvard University.

Left: A red carpet 163 feet long heralds the 1966 opening of the Metropolitan Opera House in New York.

Above left: Louis Kahn's 1964 Ahmadabad Institute of Management in India demonstrates the exportability of the modern style. Kahn was relatively unusual in using a traditional building material, brick, as a concession in to the building's location.

Above: Colonel Seifert's Centre Point building in London, is one of the more durable of 1960s' nose-thumbing modernist designs.

Left: The great disaster of modern architecture was high-rise housing which applied Le Corbusier's utopian theories at the expense of a humane environment.

Far left: The University of Sussex in Brighton, England, was one of several new universities which turned away from Oxbridge traditionalism.

Left: Simone de Beauvoir's concerns as a writer make her in many ways someone who had been waiting for the 1960s to happen. Her book *The Second Sex* (1949-53) articulated the feminist position that women are psychically repressed by men from the existentialist position whereby human beings find meaning in life by defining themselves in opposition to others.

Right: Jean-Paul Sartre and Simone de Beauvoir in Paris in 1964, the year that Sartre turned down the Nobel prize for literature for 'objective and personal reasons.'

Below right: Naom Chomsky, pioneer of structural linguistics and guardian of truth. He has dedicated himself to exposing establishment and First World deceit through a tight textual analysis of official proclamations.

Below: The psychologist B F Skinner's work is now largely discredited because it relies too heavily on rather simplistic assumptions inferred from behavioral experiments with rats. He proposed that behavior is entirely determined by environmental pressures, and that psychology should restrict itself to the study of observable behavior.

Left: Graham Greene was already an established author long before the 1960s, but some of his major concerns – social injustice and the search for a personal destiny – became those of the decade of protest.

Above: Aldous Huxley is remembered mainly today as the author of *Brave New World* (1932), a frightening vision of a future dystopic world. For the 1960s his importance lies in two books he wrote in the mid-1950s, *The Doors of Perception* (1954) and *Heaven and Hell* (1956), which chronicle his experiments with mescalin and LSD.

Above right: The man who used the 'f-word' on television, English theater critic Kenneth Tynan, pictured here in 1970 with his wife Kathleen.

Right: D H Lawrence's novel *Lady Chatterley's Lover* was finally published in an unexpurgated version in Britain after a much-publicized obscenity trial in which it was found 'Not Guilty.'

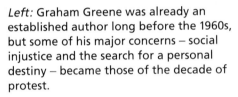

Left: Alexander Solzhenitsyn's writings caused shockwaves in the west when they first emerged in the 1960s. He exposed in the *Gulag Archipelago* the cruelty of Soviet labor camps, and contended that its source was not the monolithic malevolent state but the uncultured and desensitized mandarins of the state.

Right: Novelist Gabriel Garcia Marquez in Mexico City after escaping arrest in Colombia.

Below right: German novelist Günter Grass's exposé of the essential childishness of the conformity which allowed Nazism to prevail in prewar Germany was encapsulated in the *Tin Drum* (1958-62). He has been active in opposing the excesses of many right wing totalitarian regimes.

Below: Alexander Solzhenitsyn receiving his Nobel Prize for Literature in 1970, four years after the award was made.

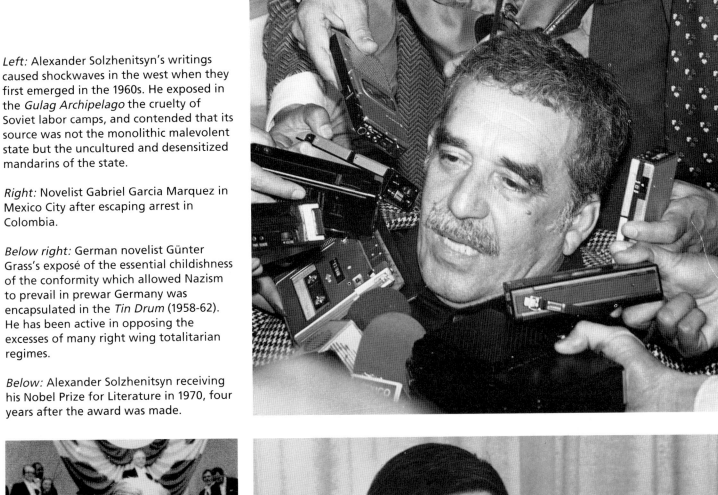

Left: William Burroughs at his typewriter in Paris. Burroughs' novels *Junkie* (1953), *Queer* (1955), and *The Naked Lunch* (1959) appealed to the disaffected 1960s' generation.

Above: American novelist Kurt Vonnegut, whose tales of World War II experiences *Slaughterhouse-Five* (1969) struck a chord with the Vietnam war generation.

Right: American poet Sylvia Plath's death by suicide in 1963 sums up for many people the bleakness of her work.

Below right: American journalist Truman Capote reached the zenith of his reputation with the 1966 publication of *In Cold Blood*.

Below: The 1960s were perfect for Norman Mailer's particular blend of inspiration and self-indulgence.

Left: Dame Margot Fonteyn and Rudolph Nureyev acknowledge the curtain calls at the Metropolitan Opera House in May 1969.

Right: Margot Fonteyn and Rudolf Nureyev rehearsing Roland Petit's new ballet *Paradise Lost* at Covent Garden, London, February 1967.

Left: Rudolf Nureyev shortly after he defected from the Soviet Union while the Leningrad Ballet was in Paris in 1961. His partner here is Maria Tallchief, and they are being directed by the Danish ballet star Erik Bruhn.

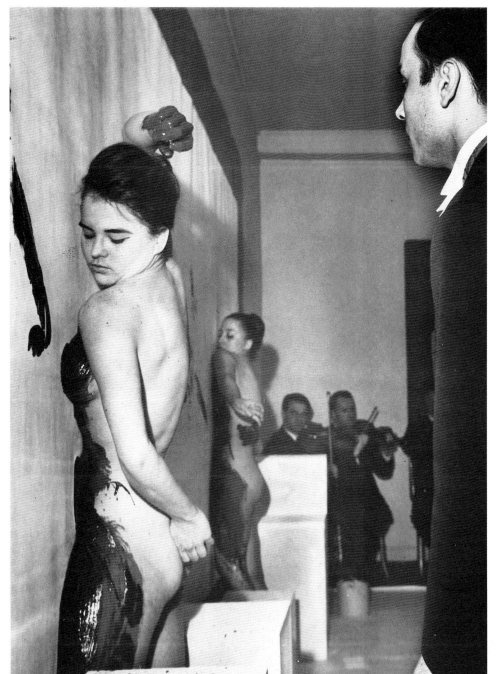

Above left: Pop artist Claes Oldenburg with one of his 'soft' sculptures, *Giant Ice Bag*.

Above: American painter Frank Stella works and does a Woody Allen impersonation at the same time.

Above right: Bulgarian-born artist Christo at the La Salita gallery in Rome with some of his 'empaquetage' sculptures, 1963.

Above, far right: One of Andy Warhol's more complex Campbell's soup-can paintings, *Campbell's Soup Can with Peeling Label*, after it was sold by New York auctioneers Parke-Bernet for $60,000.

Right: Roy Lichtenstein at work in 1964 on one of his paintings inspired by comic strips.

Left: Yves Klein turned the creation of his monochromatic paintings into a performance with naked models and a string quartet.

Overleaf: Pop art and psychedelia made the sixties a classic era for poster art. By the end of the decade the advertising industry had adopted a diluted version of the style.

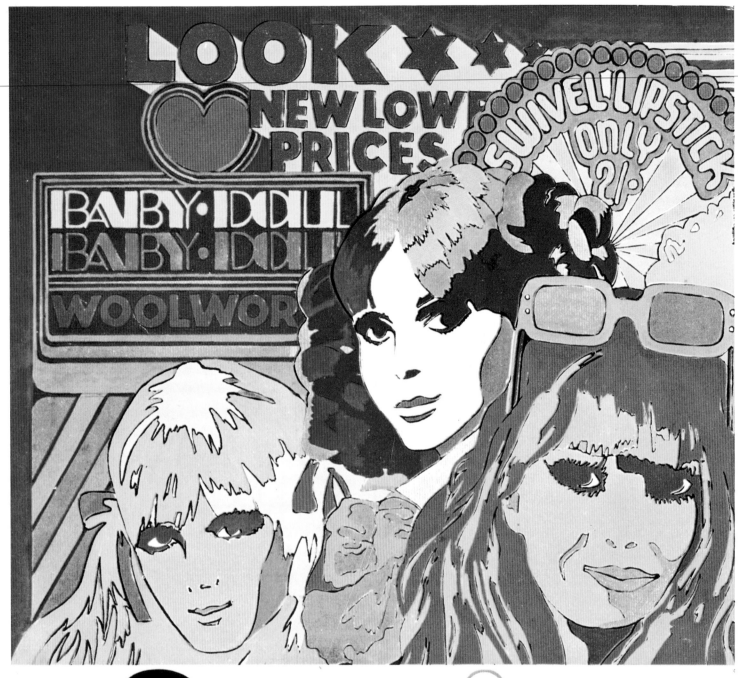

No 8.4-1   1967 © FAMILY DOG PRODUCTIONS 639 GOUGH ST. San Francisco, Calif 94102

Civil Rights

If there is one recurrent theme that pervaded all aspects of life in the sixties, it is the desire for greater freedom: freedom of expression, freedom in fashion, in music, in sexuality. But perhaps the greatest struggle for increased freedom was the one which took place in the United States, the quest for civil rights for blacks or, as they were categorized, Negroes.

For a nation which liked to call itself 'the land of the free' the United States was remarkably lacking in individual liberties for a large section of its population. Segregation on the basis of skin color was, as in South Africa, permitted and rife, particularly in the southern states, and while the fifties had seen an increase in challenges to this unacceptable status quo, it wasn't until the sixties that the mobilization of black interest groups made any meaningful impact.

Following the example of Mahatma Gandhi in the thirties, the emphasis was very much on peaceful protest, which initially took the form of sit-ins in all-white canteens and Freedom Rides on buses to challenge segregation in bus terminals. This peaceful approach was epitomized by the Rev Dr Martin Luther King, a charismatic leader who preached dignified, non-violent protest with stirring rhetoric which culminated in his 'I have a dream' speech in front of an estimated 200,000 supporters at the Lincoln Memorial in Washington DC in 1963. But King's reasonable stance was under fire on all sides.

On the one hand, militant blacks advocated a more vigorous form of protest, encouraged by such as Malcolm X, radical leader of the Black Muslims movement, who derided King's integrationist message. On the other hand was the

whole welter of prejudice and segregationist legislation so deeply ingrained in America's white establishment. Dr King was frequently arrested, charged and convicted for organizing illegal demonstrations, and it was not uncommon for a peaceful march to break out into bloodshed when its leaders were arrested and the authorities were sent in (usually by segregationist mayors or governors) to disperse the crowd. State forces often confronted protestors with bayonets fixed and batons flying. Many died.

Fortunately the civil rights movement had the backing of the decade's two Democrat presidents, John F Kennedy and Lyndon B Johnson. JFK challenged the Alabama state Governor George Wallace over his defiance of federal integration orders and sent in federal troops to safeguard the enrolment of two blacks at the University of Alabama. The education issue had come to a head when James Meredith became the first black to be admitted to the all-white University of Mississippi, sparking off a massive riot. On that occasion, too, the federal President Kennedy clashed with the state governor.

LBJ signed a number of important items of legislation which pushed back the tide of institutionalized racism in the United States: in particular the 1964 and 1968 Civil Rights Acts outlawed racial discrimination in the fields of employment, public facilities, union membership, and property and accommodation rights.

Malcolm X left his Black Muslims in 1964 and formed a more radical 'black nationalist party' which he called the Organization for Afro-American Unity, claiming ominously that 'there can be no revolution without bloodshed.' He was right, for within a year Malcolm X would be dead, victim of the Black Muslims he had once led.

In 1965 race riots spread from the south to other US cities and the murder of three civil rights workers in Alabama by the Ku Klux Klan stoked the already raging fire of racial tension.

But the issue took on a greater significance when set in a wider context. The success of black individuals across the whole cultural spectrum in America was cast into sharp relief against the prevailing injustice against blacks in general. Sidney Poitier won the Oscar for Best Actor for his part in Lilies of the Field; black athletes excelled in the Rome, Tokyo and Mexico Olympics. In 1967 the first black Supreme Court Judge, Thurgood Marshall, was sworn in; Shirley Chisholm became the first black woman elected to the House of Representatives, Edward W Brooke the first black Senator for 85 years, and so on. Against this sweeping tide of blacks' involvement in the life of the nation, resistance became more futile, but all the more concerted in spite of that.

James Meredith, of Mississippi University fame, was shot and wounded as he marched for civil rights. Dr King was less fortunate and was fatally wounded by an assassin as he was chatting with the Rev Jesse Jackson in April 1968. The national Chairman of the violent Black Panthers, Bobby Seale, was jailed for contempt of court, while the Panthers' 'Prime Minister', Stokely Carmichael, and another prominent Panther, Eldridge Cleaver, left America amid acrimonious in-fighting.

Nevertheless, the decade ended with considerable gains having been achieved in the field of civil rights, but the cost in lives and ill-will was high. Thanks to the courage and persistence of a number of key figures, both black and white, in the face of belligerence on all sides, the sixties closed with America a few steps closer to Martin Luther King's dream.

Previous pages: The authorities clamp down on a Negro youth during rioting in Elizabeth, New Jersey in 1964.

Left: Malcolm X, aggressive leader of America's Black Muslim movement, arriving in Washington DC to establish his headquarters. A one-time petty criminal, pimp, and drug addict, Malcolm X was familiar with the problems facing young blacks in urban ghettoes.

Above: Martin Luther King (wearing a white cap in the foreground) leads an estimated 1500 civil rights marchers on the penultimate leg of their trek from Selma to Montgomery, Alabama in March 1965.

Right: The bloodstained body of a looter lies in a parking lot in Los Angeles in August 1965.

MEREDITH OFF TO ENROLL;
BARNETT ACTION BLOCKED

Left: From the Alabama State Capitol in Montgomery (*top*) to the White House in Washington (*bottom*), civil rights protestors made their presence felt, despite warnings of bloodshed from nervous authorities.

Top: Ugly scenes in Birmingham, Alabama. Like so many civil rights demonstrations, this one ended in violence.

Right: James Meredith ran the gauntlet of a racist backlash to gain a degree at the all-white University of Mississippi.

Above: Some of the more than 200,000 participants in the historic 'March on Washington' on 28 August 1963.

Left: A sea of placards spells out in simple terms the demands of civil rights protestors as they make their peaceful way to the Lincoln Memorial to hear what turned out to be one of the most moving speeches ever delivered.

Below: 'I have a dream that one day this nation will rise up and live out the true meaning of its creed: "We hold these truths to be self-evident; that all men are created equal." ' Dr King delivers his famous and unforgettable speech from the Lincoln Memorial, Washington DC, 1963.

236

Above right: Grief of three mothers; their sons were civil rights workers who were killed in Mississippi in August 1964 by police officers affiliated to the Ku Klux Klan.

Above far right: Police set their dogs on protestors in Birmingham, Alabama.

Below: Flying the flag. Freedom marchers keep their spirits up as they near Montgomery, Alabama in March 1965.

Right below (inset): President Johnson receives congratulations from Dr King after signing the Civil Rights Act, 1965.

Right: Martin Luther King, whose dream ended with the assassin's bullet in Memphis, 1968. More than any other individual, King forced America to reassess its attitudes towards segregation. His mesmeric oratory inspired civil rights campaigns across the country.

Left: Lester Maddox makes a stand against the integration order imposed on him by a federal court; he wanted to keep blacks out of his restaurant.

Below: National Guardsmen confront rioting blacks with fixed bayonets in Detroit, Michigan, July 1967.

240

Left: Thomas Allen (aged three) surveys the remains of his home after the July riots in Detroit in 1967.

Below: Supreme Court Justice Thurgood Marshall became the court's first black justice on 2 October 1967.

Bottom: In Memphis the National Guard lays on tanks and bayonets for protestors as they remind Tennessee of the simple words of Martin Luther King: 'I am a man.'

Right: On 4 April 1968 Martin Luther King was shot dead. Mules drew a farm waggon bearing his coffin through Atlanta, Georgia.

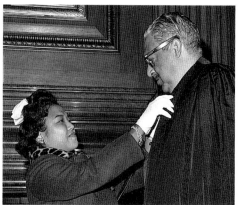

Signs of the Times

The sixties were years of great technological advance, the most memorable event being Neil Armstrong walking on the dusty surface of the moon. In 1960 John Kennedy had promised a man on the moon before the end of the decade, an objective that was achieved on 20 July 1969.

In the world of medicine the widespread availability of the contraceptive pill revolutionized women's lives, enabling them to control their bodies in a manner unprecedented. Dr Christiaan Barnard, a South African surgeon, carried out the first successful heart transplant on a human being and scientists at Stanford University created life in a test tube. Humanity, it seemed, was at last establishing a stronger influence over life and death.

Mankind could not, however, manipulate the elements, and the sixties had its share of natural disasters. Morocco and Alaska were struck by strong earthquakes, and Florence suffered horrendous floods when the River Arno burst its banks in 1966. The mining village of Aberfan in Wales suffered one of the most distressing tragedies when a slag heap collapsed on a school killing 116 children and 28 adults.

To the delight of the media, scandals plagued those in high places. In 1963 John Profumo, British minister for war, was forced to resign when it became clear that not only had he been conducting an affair with one Christine Keeler, but that a Russian naval attaché also featured among her lovers. The Profumo Affair had a devastating effect on British public opinion. People were thrilled to read (in lurid detail) about the antics of a number of highly-placed members of society with call-girls. The security risk came a distant second in the general public's enjoyment of the case.

In a similar vein, Senator Edward Kennedy's antic's aroused adverse comment in 1969 when he crashed his car. His companion, an attractive young woman called Mary Jo Kopechne, drowned as Kennedy failed in his attempts to pull her out of the waterlogged car. The authorities were not informed until eight hours after the accident, which smacked of a Kennedy cover-up. The incident cast a pall of suspicion over Edward Kennedy which has never really dissipated.

Grisly murder hit the headlines on both sides of the Atlantic. The Moors Murders were discovered in 1965 as police dug up the bodies of children buried on the moors outside Manchester. A disturbed and sadistic couple, Ian Brady and Myra Hindley, had tortured and killed a number of children, and were both sentenced to life imprisonment. In America the Manson Murders of 1969 challenged the whole hippy ethos of rejecting conventional restraints on behavior. Charles Manson, a deranged hippy, attracted a 'family' of followers over whom he exercised hypnotic control. Convinced that the Apocalypse would be precipitated by the murder of white Americans, he a bloody rampage through Los Angeles, killing eight people, including Sharon Tate, the wife of film director Roman Polanski.

All in all the sixties was a decade of extraordinary events, many of which still haunt us today.

Previous pages: In March 1964 Alaska was rocked by a tremendous earthquake which wrecked Anchorage. The tremors set off a tidal wave which swept over coastlines as far away as Hawaii and California.

Left and right: The space race between the Soviet Union and the USA was one of the more friendly areas of competition between the two countries. The Americans, shocked by the early Russian lead in space, were determined to recover the initiative in the early 1960s. In 1962 John Glenn (left, with President Kennedy) became the first man to orbit the earth three times. The Soviet cosmonaut, Yuri Gagarin (right, with Valentin Tereshkova, the first woman in space), had made the first manned flight the previous year, however.

Above: In 1966 the small Welsh mining town of Aberfan suffered an appalling tragedy when a slag heap collapsed, engulfing the town's junior school. Almost an entire generation of children was wiped out when 144 people, 116 of them children, died.

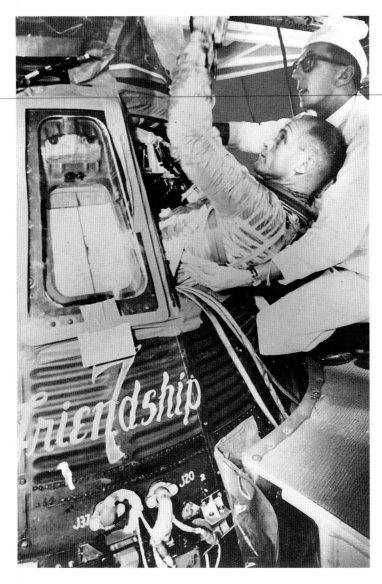

Above left: John Glenn climbs into 'Friendship 7', the spacecraft in which he orbited the earth, 1962.

Above: The Soviet space probe Ventura 4, which replaced Ventura 3, the first manmade object to reach another planet.

Left: Yuri Gagarin, the first man in space. On 12 April 1961, he piloted his craft, Vostok 1, for 108 minutes, before returning to earth.

Right: Science fiction becomes reality – the Project Mercury astronauts in 1961. Alan Shepard, the first American in space in May 1961, is left, back row; John Glenn is front row, second right.

These pages: One of the great scandals of the decade rocked the British establishment in 1963. John Profumo, the Minister for War (below), was embroiled in a situation combining two taboos: sex and national security. He had been conducting an affair with Christine Keeler, a 19-year-old call girl (right) who lived under the protection of society osteopath Stephen Ward (left). A Soviet intelligence officer Eugene Ivanov was also among Miss Keeler's lovers. Profumo denied the affair, but three months later, he admitted that he had lied to Parliament, and Stephen Ward was arrested on trumped-up charges of pimping. The salacious stories surrounding Keeler and another of Ward's protegées, Mandy Rice-Davies (below left), provided the tabloids with profit-making headlines, and produced pompous statements from members of the establishment. Rice-Davies's apposite comment when told that a man of some standing had denied her allegations, 'He would, wouldn't he', seemed to sum up the spirit of the affair.

Above: Dr Christiaan Barnard, the South African surgeon who performed the world's first heart transplant in 1967.

Left: James Watson and Francis Crick, the scientists who were awarded nobel prizes in 1962 for their work on DNA. A few years previously they had discovered the double helix shape of DNA, the coded nucleic acids which carry genetic information in all living organisms.

Above right: Not all scientific experimentation was as successful. In the late fifties a new 'wonder tranquilizer' was marketed which prevented morning sickness in pregnant women. What was unknown, was that it also caused malformation of the foetus. Before it was withdrawn in the early sixties, thalidomide was responsible for at least 5000 disabled children, many born with partially-formed limbs.

Below right and above far right: The earth itself still held some attraction for adventurers. Francis Chichester was the first man to circumnavigate the globe single-handedly in 1967, a feat for which he was knighted on his return. And Thor Heyerdahl crossed the Atlantic in a reconstruction of an ancient Egyptian papyrus-reed boat. He published his account of the 1969 'Ra Expedition' a few years later.

Left: On 8 August 1963 a gang in Britain stole £2.5 million from a mail train in a brilliantly-executed robbery that was to turn the perpetrators into folk heroes. The 30-man gang stopped the Aberdeen Express and made off with the largest sum of stolen money in British history. The bandits themselves (of whom two are pictured here, Albert Reynolds far left, and Ronnie Biggs, right) were gradually caught and given long prison sentences. The story did not end there: several, including Biggs, escaped, and were pursued for many years by Scotland Yard. Biggs still lives in exile in Brazil.

Above and below: A far more serious case occupied the Manchester police in the first half of the decade. In a series of unexplained incidents, several young children disappeared from their Lancashire homes. In 1965 a sadistic couple, Myra Hindley (below left) and Ian Brady (below right) were found to have tortured children to death, recording their screams before burying their bodies on the moors. Both were sentenced to life imprisonment.

Left: An earthquake, described as a 'minor tremor' by the authorities, destroyed parts of Skopje, Yugoslavia in July 1963.

Below left: The Moroccan earthquake of 1960 was far more serious. Several thousand people died when the resulting tidal wave and fire wrecked Agadir.

Right and below right: One of the great cultural tragedies of the decade was the result of a natural disaster. In 1966 torrential rain caused the River Arno to burst its banks. Florence was flooded, the narrow streets turned into rivers, many architectural gems damaged and priceless frescoes and works of art destroyed.

Below: The Biafran civil war in Nigeria produced untold suffering from 1967. Not only was the nation embroiled in bitter conflict, but the country was also stricken with famine.

In a decade of upheaval, and at a time when many colonies sought their freedom from their former colonial masters, the British royal family remained a constant.

Above: The royal family in 1965. From left, Prince Charles, Princess Anne, Prince Philip, Prince Andrew, and the Queen holding Prince Edward.

Left: The Queen, with her younger children, Prince Andrew and the infant Prince Edward, in 1964. The royal family enjoyed something of a baby boom during the early sixties. The Queen's sister Princess Margaret married in 1960 and had two children by 1964, and their cousins, the Duke and Duchess of Kent and Princess Alexandra produced five children by 1965.

Far left: The Queen with the Australian Prime Minister Bob Menzies. Menzies was criticized during his premiership (1963-6) for laying too much stress on Australia's links with Britain and the USA.

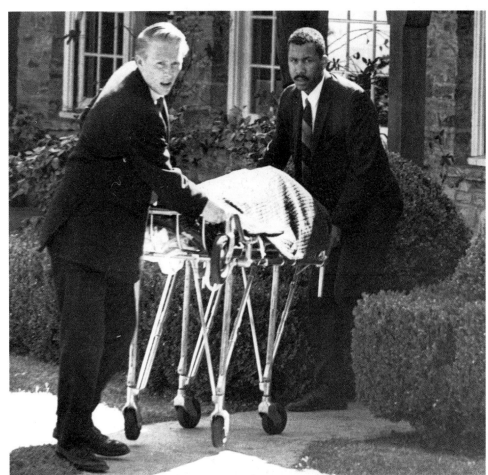

Above, left and right: In 1969 the Charles Manson murders shocked the world. On 8 August 1969, Manson and his followers hacked to death five people including Roman Polanski's wife Sharon Tate (left & right). .

Below: The sole surviving Kennedy brother, Teddy, was involved in a dubious car accident at Chappaquidick in 1969. His companion drowned after Kennedy failed to pull her from his immersed car.

In 1961 President Kennedy pledged that America would put a man on the moon by the end of the decade, promising that 'No single project will be more impressive to mankind.' When the dream became reality on 20 July 1969, the television viewing figures alone made it clear that Kennedy had not been exaggerating. Three astronauts (pictured left, L-R) Neil Armstrong, Michael Collins, and Edwin 'Buzz' Aldrin took off from Cape Kennedy on 17 July in Apollo 11 (above left). Three days later, Armstrong bounced gently on to the moon's Sea of Tranquility, uttering his now-famous words, 'That's one small step for a man, one giant leap for mankind'. Watched by a television audience of 600 million, the moon landing was as much an historic TV spectacular as a great exploratory and scientific achievement.

Epilogue

The 1960s has been saddled with more soubriquets than almost any other decade. The swinging sixties, the decade of liberation, of protest, of violence and assassination, of cold war and confrontation, of civil rights and feminism – the mythologization of the decade knows no bounds.

Perhaps the single most burning and controversial issue, and one that has continued to reverberate, was the Vietnam War. Beginning in 1959/60, the conflict escalated to a point where, at its height in 1967/68, there were over half a million US troops in Vietnam. Peace talks began in 1968, but US forces only finally left South Vietnam in March 1973. By 1975 South Vietnamese morale had collapsed, and after reunification in 1976 more than 750,000 people fled the country as refugees.

On the world stage the 1960s saw the Cold War reach its peak, with the U2 skyplane scandal, the Bay of Pigs fiasco and the missile crisis in Cuba each in turn bringing the two superpowers to the point of armed confrontation, and the world to the brink of nuclear war. The building of the Berlin Wall in 1961 symbolized a divided world and gave Churchill's Iron Curtain metaphor tangible and tragic form.

In the rest of the decade, world attention shifted to the upheavals of the Cultural Revolution in China, which claimed a major role in world politics in subsequent years but remained a rigidly Communist state, greeting any sign of liberation with the ferocious repression seen in Tiananmen Square in 1990. The process of decolonization continued, with growing numbers of Third World countries achieving independence and UN status. Economic stability was another problem altogether, however, and the period since 1970 has seen the disparity between the industrialized West and the Third World becoming increasingly contentious.

Then there were the Swinging Sixties, when rock music seemed to rule the world and pop musicians wielded as much influence as statesmen. When British Prime Minister Harold Wilson announced the award of CBEs to the Beatles, the Establishment rocked on its heels. The young had acquired purchasing power and suddenly youth culture was a force to be reckoned with, in politics as well as music and fashion. The mini-skirted dolly bird screaming with enthusiasm for her favorite pop group is a perennial sixties image, while the Merseybeat, the folk movement, Motown blues, all encapsulate the sixties sound.

As the decade of protest and liberation, the 1960s saw many social and political groups finding a new voice. The anti-nuclear movement responded with growing concern and increasingly radical action to the worldwide proliferation of nuclear technology. The general anti-authoritarian trend was part and parcel of the youth rebellion, which expessed itself in serious student unrest in both Europe and the US, culminating in 'les évenements' in Paris in 1968 and focusing on the anti-war issue and black civil rights in the US.

Another movement which took off in the 1960s, and which exposed the contradictions inherent within the liberal *laissez-faire* consensus, was women's rights. Feminists pointed out that what constituted liberation for some represented repression and exploitation for others. First expressed as a problem of individual self-determination, this dilemma has since come increasingly to dominate the world political and economic scene.

Previous pages: Naked terror. One of the most enduring images of the Vietnam War. The victims, stripped naked by a napalm strike that burned their clothes, flee for their lives in South Vietnam.

Below left: When refugees flooded out of Vietnam at the end of the war in 1975, aircraft carriers and other ships were unable to cope with the large numbers of rescue helicopters many of which had to be heaved overboard to make way for incoming evacuating aircraft.

Below: Fall-out from the Vietnam War. The boat people flee from their beleaguered country in the early seventies.

Right: The Biafran War in Nigeria ended in 1970 with the surrender of secessionist Biafra. Here, the new federal leader Maj. Gen. Yakubu Gowon addresses a press conference in Lagos.

Above: Leonid Brezhnev and Muammar Ghadaffi, two world leaders who rose to prominence in the sixties and became the West's *bêtes noires* in the seventies.

Left: Jane Fonda at a press conference following her confrontation with the authorities over the American Indian issue: about 160 Indians had tried to turn Fort Lawton into an Indian culture center.

Above right: The five-day Isle of Wight pop festival in 1970, attended by some 250,000 people, was a throw-back to the sixties mega-festivals, such as Newport and Woodstock. The presence of swastika-bearing Hell's Angels led to a police raid to confiscate offensive weapons.

Below right: The antiwar protests continue. In 1970 National Guardsmen fired tear gas canisters at students on the Kent State University Campus in Ohio . . . as well as live ammunition. Four were killed.

Overleaf, left and right: The sixties established rallies and demonstrations as bona fide means of political and social protest.

Left: Bob Dylan, the inspiration behind many sixties' supergroups, carried on performing to adulatory fans for decades. He has explored many musical paths since, but his output has never quite surpassed the unforgettable music and lyrics he produced in the mid-sixties.

Right: Janis Joplin, one of the most powerful female rock singers of the 1960s. She had an amazing blues voice, but her persistent attempts to keep up with the traditional lifestyles of the sixties' rock star was to be the death of her.

Acknowledgments

Designer: David Eldred
Production: Nicki Giles

The publisher would like to thank the following institutions for supplying the pictures used on the pages noted below:

Allsport USA: 152 below
The Bettmann Archive: 8, 9 below, 11 bottom pair, 12 below, 13, 17 below, 18 top, 22 both, 23 below, 24 both, 25 both, 26 both, 27 both, 28, 29 all 3, 30 all 3, 31 both, 32 below, 33 top right, 34 below, 36 top, 37 both, 38 both, 39 both, 41 below, 42 all 3, 43, 44-45, 47 below, 48, 49 both, 50 both, 51 both, 52 top, 53 below left, 55 top, 56-7 all 3, 58 top, 59 below, 61 below, 62 both, 63 all 3, 64 both, 65 both, 67 both, 68-9 all 4, 71 top, 72 below, 76, 77 top, 78

top, 82 top, 86 top, 87 both, 96 both, 97, 98-9 all 4, 100-1 all 3, 102-103 all 4, 104-5 all 3, 106 both, 108-9 all 3, 110-111 all 4, 112-113 all 3, 114-115 all 4, 116-117 all 3, 118-119, 120 left, 121, 123 below right, 124, 125, 142 all 3, 148 all 3, 150, 151, 152 top, 153 top, 154 all 3, 155 both, 158-159, 160 both, 161, 162 both, 163 all 3, 164 all 3, 165 both, 166 top left and below, 167 below, 168 all 3, 169, 170, 171 both, 172 both, 173 both, 174 both, 175 both, 177 both, 178-179 all 4, 180-181 all 4, 182-183 all 3, 184-185 all 3, 186-187 all 4, 188-189 all 4, 191 all 3, 194, 195 top, 208 all 3, 210 below, 214, 215 all 3, 216, 217 top pair, 218, 219, 220, 221 all 4, 222 both, 223, 224 top pair, 225 all 3, 228-229, 230-231 all 3, 232-233 all 4, 234-235 all 3, 236-237, 237 below, 238 both, 240 all 3, 241, 242-243, 245 all 3, 245 left pair, 247, 248 all 3, 249, 250-251 all 5, 252-253 all

6, 254-255 all 5, 257 both, 258, 259 below and top right, 260 all 3, 261, 265 top, 266 below, 267 both
Harry Benson Black Star: 53 top
BPL: 6-7, 9 top, 10 all 3, 14-15, 16, 18 below, 19 both, 20 both, 21, 23 top, 33 below, 34 top, 35 both, 36, 40 all 3, 41 top, 47 top, 52 below, 53 below right, 54 top, 54 below, 66 both, 70, 71 top, 73 both, 75-6, 77 below, 78 below, 79 all 3, 80 both, 81 both, 82 below, 83 both, 84-85 all 4, 86 below, 88 both, 89 both, 90-91 all 4, 92-93 all 4, 94-95, 107, 120 right, 127 both, 128, 129 both, 130 below right, 140 top, 141, 142 all 3, 143 all 3, 144 all 3, 145 all 3, 146 both, 147 both, 149, 153 below, 157 top, 190, 192-193, 195 below, 197 top, 198 both, 200 below, 201 below, 202 below, 205 both, 206 top, 210 top, 211 both, 212 top, 237 top, 239, 246 top right, 256,

259 top left, 262-263, 264, 265 below, 266 top, 267
Globe: 136-137
Hulton-Deutsch Collection: 12 top, 45 below, 156 both, 157 below, 213 top, 217 below
Robert Hunt Picture Library: 48 top
Israeli Govt Press Office: 46, 58 below, 59 top, 60 both, 61 top
National Film Archive: 196 both, 197 below, 199 both, 200, 201 top, 202 top, 203 both, 204, 206 below, 207 all 3
Peter Newark's Pictures: 32
Pictorial Press: 166 top right, 224 below
Redferns: 2-3, 122 both, 123 top and below left, 126 130 top and below left, 131, 132, 133, 134-135 all 5, 138 all 3, 139, 140 bottom pair, 268
Topham Picture Source: 32 top left, 213 top
Vintage Magazine Company: 4-5 all 4, 11 top, 17 top, 167 top, 176, 226, 227, 269 below